SOMETHING HAS GONE WRONG

SOMETHING HAS GONE WRONG

Dealing with the Brighton Bomb

STEVE RAMSEY

Biteback Publishing

First published in Great Britain in 2018 by
Biteback Publishing Ltd
Westminster Tower
3 Albert Embankment
London SE1 7SP
Copyright © Steve Ramsey 2018

ISBN 978-1-78590-336-6

10 9 8 7 6 5 4 3 2 1

A CIP catalogue record for this book is available from the British Library.

Set in Sabon LT by Adrian McLaughlin

Printed and bound in Great Britain by
CPI Group (UK) Ltd, Croydon CR0 4YY

CONTENTS

FOREWORD

The events of the early hours of Friday 12 October 1984 will remain sharply remembered by those who lived through them, or who saw the television coverage of the escape of some and the rescue of others from the ruins of the Grand Hotel, Brighton that morning.

My recollection of events from the moment the IRA bomb that was intended to murder Prime Minister Thatcher exploded to departing the scene by ambulance are seared into my memory, but thereafter I lapsed into unconsciousness.

Steve Ramsey's book is not only a graphic account of the events of that morning as it was seen through the eyes of the victims; it also details how the emergency services, police, hospital staff and the civil service were brought into what became an immensely complex operation. Initially there was no time for a textbook top-down operation, with senior staff taking control and issuing instructions to those on the scene.

As Ramsey's book sets out, it was those dealing with events on the scene at the Grand Hotel and the Royal Sussex Hospital who took the decisions, in line with the military adage that no plan can ever withstand contact with reality.

At the scene, the policy that only the bomb squad could enter the immediate environment of a terrorist bombing until the possibility of a second, booby-trap weapon had been explored was ignored in order to rescue survivors.

At the Royal Sussex Hospital, it was impossible to refuse to identify casualties to the media, since live TV had broadcast the rescue of casualties as they were carried or stumbled out of the wreckage.

In many ways, however, the most important part of the book is its account of the meticulous work of the police forensic and investigative teams. They patiently worked to follow a tortuous path of clues which led to the identification, arrest and conviction of the IRA terrorist operative Patrick Magee, who had planted the bomb.

Sadly, those who planned, financed and commissioned the crime had not been brought to justice before they were guaranteed immunity by Prime Minister Blair.

What has stood out ever since the Brighton bombing was the response of Prime Minister Thatcher. Despite such a close brush with death, only six hours later – absolutely as scheduled – she was on the platform at the Brighton Conference Centre to address not only her party, but the world. The message was clear. Cowardly terrorism had failed; courage and democracy had triumphed. The world took note. I was still barely conscious, but already the machinery of government was moving into action. My Department of Trade and Industry private secretaries, Andrew Lansley and Callum McCarthy, were soon setting up office in Brighton. After my wife and I were transferred to Stoke Mandeville Hospital two weeks later by helicopter, I began to resume control of my department from my hospital bed.

By Christmas I had had more than enough of hospital life, and discharged myself, having been invited to spend Christmas at Chequers with the Prime Minister and Denis Thatcher. Although I did return to Stoke Mandeville for Christmas lunch – traditional hospital style – with my wife. It was an extraordinary event.

The roast turkey, Brussels sprouts and roast potatoes arrived on a trolley from the operating theatre. The three consultant surgeons went to work carving the turkey with surgical skills. I began to laugh.

'What is so funny?' one of them asked. 'You three,' I replied. 'Look at yourselves – two Jews and a Palestinian – not a Christian amongst you!'

I think I learned something that day.

Indeed, the events recounted by Steve Ramsey suggest that we can, almost all of us, both do more and learn more under the stress of terrible events than we had ever thought likely.

Stress can be a powerful learning tool.

NORMAN TEBBIT
May 2017

CHAPTER ONE

THANK YOU FOR COMING

'That's definitely not thunder,' said one police officer who had heard the noise, which came from the direction of Brighton's Grand Hotel. The Prime Minister and many of her colleagues, in town for the Conservative Party conference, were inside. The air was dusty, and there were pieces of the hotel on the seafront. It was 2.54 a.m. on Friday 12 October 1984.

A police vehicle outside the Brighton Centre, next to the Grand, was shaken by the shockwave, and hit by dust so thick that 'it was almost like someone had thrown a blanket over the van,' policeman Paul Parton recalls. 'I think my immediate thought was, gas explosion, or something like that. And then someone obviously said, "Oh, IRA." And it was like, "What, in Brighton?"'

Harvey Thomas, the conference organiser, came to in mid-air. 'When you dream you're flying through space, you kind of brush asteroids and things off,' he says. 'But, in this case, they were bouncing off me, I was bouncing off them, and I realised: this is real.'

Norman Tebbit,* the Trade and Industry Secretary, had time to notice the chandelier in his room swinging and to tell his wife Margaret, 'it's a bomb!' before the room they were in collapsed, and they became part of an 'avalanche' of rubble.[1]

At Brighton police station, about a mile away on John Street, Sergeant Paddy Tomkins 'heard the detonation. And then a couple of seconds later, the Tannoy directed all staff to respond.' The connection was obvious.

Slightly further away, at Preston Circus fire station, a message came through that the Grand's fire alarm was ringing. The message didn't say why.[2] Station officer Fred Bishop thought it was probably a false alarm; someone had perhaps set it off as a prank to wake all the ministers up and make them stand outside in the cold.

---

* He is now Lord Tebbit. All titles and ranks and job roles given throughout this book are those held at the time.

'And so that was how we turned out,' Bishop says. 'And that was all we knew on the way down. So, when we actually got there, it was a great surprise to us to see what we saw.'

'I remember jumping out the back of the van and the ground was covered in rubble, bricks, broken bricks, bits of railing off the front of the hotel and everything,' policeman Paul Parton says.

> And you could taste the dust and the mess. It was all up your nose and everything, and it was everywhere. And course you're trying to make your way forward to help people, and you've got eyes full of muck and stuff.
>
> You couldn't see anything. In your mind you knew where the front of the building was, so you naturally move forward, gingerly. Well, you couldn't run, because of the state of the debris on the floor. And there's always that thing in your head – what are you going to find? You don't know what you're going to find. You just move forward and deal with what comes up.
>
> As we got closer and the dust was starting to settle, you could see [a policeman] laying on the ground, being supported by other policemen, people

screaming, hanging off balconies, alarm bells ringing, water pouring out of broken pipes, and you could see the people up on the balcony. It was horrific, insomuch as, where do you go first?

'The rubble covered the front door and the main part of the front hall,' says PC Simon Parr.

People were going in through windows, getting people out, there were people in ball gowns there, there were nurses nearby who'd been at a dinner and they were ripping their evening dresses to bandage the walking wounded as they were coming out. I remember the white and red dust. Everybody was covered in dust, because it was such a big hotel and such an old building. I remember just the incongruous nature of people in dinner suits and evening dresses, with blood on them, literally staggering as they were helped out through the windows and side doors.

As police officers in particular, everyone thinks you'll be calm and know what to do. Well, of course, I don't think any of us had ever seen anything like it. But the basic instincts of policing are to get people out.

'Here – it's suddenly got misty,' said one of fire officer Fred Bishop's colleagues, as their vehicle turned onto the seafront. Bishop recalls:

> As we drove along the seafront, we suddenly became aware that this mist, as we thought it was... 'That's not quite mist.' And suddenly we saw sheets, and pillowcases probably, and curtains and all sorts of material, hanging onto the lights that go along the seafront.
>
> As soon as we stopped, obviously, we had a job to do. And I remember a policeman being there and I said to him, 'What actually happened?' And he was completely foxed, really, because he said, 'Um, it just went bang.' And he was kind of standing there thinking, 'What am I supposed to do?' He was really confused, poor chap.

'At that point, we still didn't know it was a bomb,' Bishop says. The brigade rules were that 'if there was a bomb, or a suspected bomb, or bomb explosion, we were supposed to park two streets away, maintain radio silence, let the police deal with it, and the bomb squad, unless there was a fire.

He continues:

So I sent a couple of my crew to circumvent the building, go right round the building, just to check if they could see any fire at all. Which, they just ran round and came back within a few moments, 'There's no fire, boss.' At that point I said, 'Something dreadful has happened here. It may well have been a bomb, an explosion. It could have been a car outside, you know, car bomb. It could have been anything. So I can't officially order you to go in, because we don't know.

And I point out, there are going to be dangers inside the building, and I said, 'I'm going in to find out what the problem is, as much as I can, and sort out the rescues.' Because, obviously, looking at the debris and how it had all fallen, there were going to be people trapped, there were going to be dead bodies. And of course, all the guys on the watch said, 'If you're going in, we're coming with you, we're volunteering.' Which was great for me, because I didn't have to illegally order them into the building.

To me, I had no choice. We had to go in. That was part of our duty. When I joined the fire service, they gave us a sense of responsibility, and they always said that your first responsibility is to save life.

> If you lose a building, it burns down, we can rebuild it. You save a life first.
>
> They said [later], 'If you'd have known there was another bomb, would you have done the same things?' And I said, 'Yes, I would have done. The bomb might go off, and we're subject to it and get killed. But I always look on the bright side – [what if] we got all the people out that were trapped, get everybody away from the building, and then it goes off?'

It was clear to Bishop that he'd need significant backup, so he put back a message asking for several more engines, and, he recalls, 'as many ambulances as you can get'. He expected that the person he spoke to would say, surprisedly, 'Would you repeat that message?' He was right.

Grabbing someone who was nearby, Bishop asked, 'Sorry, are you hotel staff?'

'Yes.'

'Do you know how many people were in your hotel at the time?'

'Well, I know that there were 300 [guests].'[3]

Bishop recalls: 'So I put back that there are 300 persons as yet unaccounted for. I said there is a number obviously trapped, and there may be some who've been fatally injured. And then we just basically entered the building and started searching.'

'I was quite sure for the first five or ten minutes I was going to die,' says conference organiser Harvey Thomas. But then he realised that he was, or appeared to be, in a fairly stable position. 'And there was ten tons of rubble on me, so I couldn't do anything. And I heard the [alarm] bells, so I thought, all I can do is lie here, and sooner or later someone's going to come and find me. So I just had to lie there. It was jolly cold.'

Norman Tebbit was also trapped. He knew that he was badly injured, and thought that, like some victims of an earlier bombing in Beirut, he and his wife might be in the rubble for days before rescuers reached them. He told her not to call out for help just yet.

'You just sort of emphasised to yourself that you have to conserve what energy you had,' he says now. 'It was no good shouting for help when there's no one to hear. Wait until you hear somebody who might be able to hear you.' He held Margaret's hand, listened out for rescuers and wondered, he later wrote, 'how many other survivors there were'.[4]

Margaret Thatcher had been in the lounge of the Grand's Napoleon Suite, with her principal private secretary, Robin Butler. Hearing the explosion, Butler had initially thought it was a car bomb outside.

The first thing I said to her was, 'I think you ought to come away from the windows.' And the first thing she said to me was, 'I must see if Denis is alright.' And so she opened the door to the bedroom, which was in darkness, because Denis had been asleep. And you could hear the sounds of falling masonry, of course.

Butler later wrote that he 'paused in the sitting room, wondering what I should say to the tribunal of inquiry if she was killed by the collapsing building. To my relief she and Denis emerged almost immediately, Denis pulling on some clothes over his pyjamas.'[5]

'We went out into the corridor,' Butler says now.

One remembers that the light was still on. We looked up the corridor, and there was what looked like smoke coming out from under the door of the next door suite, which I knew was Geoffrey Howe's suite. And so I thought a bomb had been put in his room. His special-branch man was running against and trying to kick down the door.

Mrs Thatcher went to the nearby secretaries' room, where speechwriter Ronald Millar saw her 'sitting on an upright chair, very still,' he recalled in his memoirs. 'At length she murmured, "I think that was an assassination attempt, don't you?"'[6]

'Every door that was closed had to be knocked, banged, and if it was locked, kicked open, broken open,' says deputy chief fire officer Peter Rodgers. 'Every room. And hopefully a systematic search of the floors. Whilst down at the bottom, where we suspected people were trapped because of the collapse of the building, specific work was going on down there to try and locate people.'

The explosion had dislodged a heavy chimney stack, which had come crashing through the floors, punching a lift-shaft-type hole through the building, creating a large pile of rubble at the bottom. Rescuers could hear two people calling for help, fairly near the top of this pile, fireman Keith Ring recalls.

> So it was a matter of moving debris about, to try and gain a bit better access, and then lowering firefighters down on lines, or ropes as you'd know them. There'd be about six of us, on one of the lines, holding the firefighter who was working on the rubble pile, from above, so that if the rubble pile suddenly dropped further, we would just be able to pull him, he would just be left suspended. We still

had no real idea at that time how many people were likely to be in the pile.

His colleague Paul Robb recalls that 'everyone thought there'd be hundreds buried underneath it. We were expecting an awful lot more casualties, an awful lot. Everyone was thinking that.'

'There were some nasty moments' while Norman Tebbit and his wife lay trapped in the rubble, he later said.[7]

We could hear water running; we didn't know where that was or whether we were going to find water rising about us. I suffered a couple of very strong electric shocks, when the people beginning to attempt the rescue cut through a cable which was still live. That was a moment when I did think I was dying, but the pain went away and I realised I wasn't dead... I thought, 'that's it, is it?' Then thought, 'Oh, you fool, you're still alive.'

'My phone went at home,' says Detective Superintendent Bernie Wells.

A voice said, 'This is the ops-room Inspector, a bomb has gone off in the Grand Hotel.' Well, it was only that previous evening we'd celebrated what a good [conference] week we'd had, how well it had all gone. I said, 'Come on, it's a wind up.' He said, 'It's not, and I can't stay talking to you because I've got a lot of people to phone.' And now it's beginning to dawn on me, this is for real.

And, well, I can remember getting up and getting dressed, but I was in some sort of trance, because I'm thinking: 'Goodness gracious.' Bear in mind Sussex [Police] had never had a bomb explosion before, ever.

PC Chris Cox was also woken by a phone call. 'Come to work; there's been an incident,' he recalls being told.

'What, no...'

'Come to work, there's been an incident. Goodbye.'

He went to Brighton police station.

Up to the first floor, which is where the uniform people lived and where all my folks were. And there was nobody there. And I thought, 'What's going on? What is happening?' So there were some tables where we used to sit and eat sandwiches in the middle of the night. And there were sandwiches, on the tables, with bites out of the corners. And

half-drunk cups of coffee or tea or something.
It was straight out of a cartoon. And I thought,
'Christ, that must have been urgent. Whatever it is,
something's happened, desperately'. At least you'd
finish your sandwich for most things. I wandered
round thinking, 'What the bloody hell's happening?'

There were coachloads of police officers at Butlin's in
Bognor Regis, about twenty-five miles away. They'd been
stationed there for the conference, spending the days
on standby in Brighton, apparently in case of miners'
strike-related disturbances. When the information about
the bombing came through – once their chief superintendent had been persuaded it was for real – the troops
were roused. 'A bomb's gone off at Brighton, full uniform,
ten minutes, coach,' PC Tony Gilks was told.

'It was just pandemonium, everybody getting rallied
up, onto coaches, and away as quickly as possible,' police
admin officer David Champion says. 'As soon as there
were enough police officers in uniform, didn't matter
whether it was their coach or anybody else's coach, as
they filled up, the coaches just went off and off and off.'

Met officer Mark Stanford recalls: 'There was a guy
holding a clipboard-type thing, near the gate, and was
shouting like a call sign, so we knew who were on their way.

And then we just blue lighted it into Brighton.' There was a radio on the coach, and 'everybody literally was craning their heads to listen. You had this silence. You didn't need to ask anything; you waited to be told or listened.'

The mood on Tony Gilks's coach 'was very subdued. One, you just don't know whether colleagues have been killed, as well as anyone else. We didn't know what we were going to face.'

Detective Sergeant Michael Colacicco, from the Met Police's 'C13' forensics team, who were bomb-scene specialists, was phoned during the night.

'Are you Mike Colacicco? Are you on the callout team?'

'Yes.'

'Can you come in?'

'Who are you and what do you want?'

'I can't give you any more information. Can you just come in?'

Colacicco recalls:

> I put in the car, it was a black canvas bag which contained the basic kit that we would take to any incident, which was steel boots, hardhats, overalls, whatever. Got to the outside of the yard, and you could tell that something big had happened, because of the amount of cars that were arriving and going,

blue lights and whatever. And went up to the [C13 area]. At the sort of time I arrived, to see someone else there would be unusual, other than the one guy who's on nights. And it was buzzing, there were people coming in all the time.

The instructions were 'callout team, put together enough people to go to a bomb scene'. They weren't told what the scene was, or where it was, Colacicco recalls.

But we were told there was a Green Goddess down in the car park below. Which again was unusual, because we'd normally go in our own cars. So we got in the Green Goddess and we were driving out towards the M23, and we were picked up by an escort of motorbike outriders and cars, and the driver didn't know, other than that we were going to Brighton. We had no communication, to tell us what we were going to.

When Detective Superintendent Bernie Wells got to the scene, he was approached by journalists. One of them asked: 'Do you think it's a TPU?'*

---

* Time and Power Unit.

And I didn't know what a TPU was. And I'm saying,
'I can't say anything at this stage, I've just arrived
at the scene, I've no idea what... it could be a gas
explosion.' Because I'm looking at the big gaping
hole at the front of the hotel, and there's debris
everywhere, and honestly, for a little while I was
thinking, 'God, what on earth are we going to do?'
Because I'd had no experience of it.

Margaret Thatcher's security people were keen to get her
out of the building, No. 10 official Sir David Wolfson
says, 'because if there's one bomb, there could be two
bombs.' Charles Moore's biography of Thatcher refers
to 'about twenty minutes of confusion in which people
debated where the Prime Minister should go in Brighton
for her protection'.[8]

Much of the delay, Sussex policeman Allan Neil suggests,
was 'just a matter of getting it organised'. For example,
transport had to be arranged. And someone had to be sent
to sweep a nearby multi-storey car park, 'because anybody
up there with a firearm [would have] full view of the back
door.' Neil wanted 'policemen every yard, to make sure
she gets out. So it took time. But I have no idea how long
it took. It took too long, in my mind.'

Mrs Thatcher later said that she had been 'more worried

for other people than frightened, and very, very conscious that there was now an acutely difficult situation, that we must stay absolutely calm and think about the best thing to do.'[9] She consoled a secretary, saying 'it's probably a bomb, but don't worry, dear'.[10] She went and asked after the people who'd been in the foyer. And she apparently greeted fire officer Fred Bishop by saying: 'Thank you for coming.'

Tory Party treasurer Lord McAlpine claimed in his memoirs that, before escorting Mrs Thatcher out, 'the police sent out of the hotel a double, in case there were marksmen hiding nearby.'[11] Geoffrey Howe's protection officer, David Bard, says: 'I have no knowledge of that, but I would take it with a pinch of salt. I didn't volunteer.'

'In the chaos outside the hotel, rumours had begun spreading that Margaret Thatcher had been killed,' MP Jonathan Aitken later wrote. 'Then the cry went up, "Maggie's safe!" Such was the relief that strangers shook hands, and clasped each other's shoulders – but in silence.'[12]

'A message came through that there had been this bomb,' says Sir Robert Armstrong, head of the Home Civil Service.

> I was at home. The message didn't say whether [Mrs Thatcher] had survived or been wounded

or been killed. I really thought – thought quite extraordinarily quickly, when I look back on it – what would have to be done if she'd been killed, what immediately would have had to be done, to carry on the government, the appointment of an interim Prime Minister and all that, who I should have to talk to, the Queen's private secretary, talk to people in government.

They say that there are some circumstances in which your life goes before you very fast. It was a bit like that, everything seemed to be speeded up. Then, of course, the telephone rang and it was Robin Butler, ringing to say that she was alright. So I went back to sleep.

Mrs Thatcher and some other VIPs were taken to Brighton police station, an ugly five-storey building on John Street. While a superintendent made tea, there was a discussion, 'and it was decided, or Maggie decided, that everyone went back to their country places, and attended at nine o'clock the next day, at the conference centre,' police protection officer David Bard recalls.

Some people [were] suggesting that they abandoned the conference. And she sat upon that straight away, said: 'No way. We are continuing. They don't beat us.'

I think the atmosphere was, 'what was going to happen the next day', more than anything. We weren't sort of saying, 'Oh, dear me', because we didn't know people had been killed or anything. We weren't looking back, we were looking forward, at what, where we were going. She was most insistent that it was seen that the Conservative Party carried its head high at nine o'clock.*

'Whilst we were in [the hotel], the word came around, there may be more bombs in the building,' senior fire officer Peter Rodgers says. 'We knew we'd got numbers and numbers of people trapped in there, and basically what happened, without anybody issuing any orders, the rescuers more or less looked at each other and got on with it, carried on. Because what was the alternative?'

His colleague Fred Bishop says:

I had to go out of the building and come back in again on the other side. And as I went into the doorway, there was an attaché case parked in the

---

* The conference's start time was actually 9.30 a.m.

doorway, and that's the first time I thought, 'Oh dear, is that another device?' And there was a policeman nearby, so I called him over. I said, 'That could be another device, your problem, carry on.' Just left him to it.

'There was a surveyor, as I recall, who said the building's going to fall down,' says Met officer Alan Burt. 'And everyone said [dismissively], "Yeah, jolly good, thanks."'

The Royal Sussex County Hospital had gone into major-incident mode soon after the explosion. Staff had been called in; a consultant had gone around discharging anyone he could; a medical registrar had gone to the scene to send back information about incoming patients; a triage system had been set up, to direct people to one of three areas for treatment, depending on the seriousness of their condition. This was important, A&E consultant Carlos Perez-Avila says, to make sure no one got lost 'in the heat of the battle, so to speak'. It was unclear at first how many victims they'd have, and how serious their injuries would be.

'It did not seem that long a time,' says conference organiser Harvey Thomas, who was apparently trapped in the rubble for two and a half hours. 'I just heard the bells ringing, and then, when I heard voices, I tried to call out, "Help! Help!"' But water was leaking from above him, over his face, and he could only manage a somewhat muffled 'Hilp!'

> I thought, I sound like some kind of dog. And I thought, that's exactly what I ought to sound like – firemen will break their necks to save a dog in this country. A dog or a horse, they'll break their necks to save them. I thought, that's good, so I went, 'Hilp, hilp!' And I remember thinking, thank goodness I wasn't French, and had to remember what tense to yell out help in.
>
> And, so I called out, and then I heard somebody say, 'Quiet, quiet; there's somebody alive down there.' That, I understand, was about forty-five minutes after the bomb went off. So I was awake for the whole time, but I didn't feel it was all that long a time. It went quite quickly, the two and a half hours.
>
> The truth is – I know it's terribly dull – but the truth is it was a different era. I was alive, just, during the bombing, the Blitz, on London. I remember as a tiny boy driving in a London bus and hearing a Doodlebug, Hitler's flying bombs, coming over the top and the engine cutting out and us all diving for cover. And [in] those days we were a different

group of people. We didn't faff around and we didn't make such a fuss. And, so, as far as I was concerned, 'Great, they've found me, I've got to lie in here till they get me out.'

The only thing that did worry me – I say worry me, it didn't seriously worry me, but it made me think, 'Oi, what's going on?' – was when they said, 'Hey, we've got to saw through this thing.' 'Hey, be careful, it's my leg down there.' [A rescuer] said, 'Oh it's alright, it's an air-saw.' And, for those few moments, I thought of it as being air doing the sawing, powerful air jets or something. 'Wait a minute…' And at that point I said, 'Just be careful.'

At least one member of the press had been inside the Grand Hotel at 2.54 a.m.; others arrived before the scene had been properly cordoned off. They were a 'nuisance', one rescuer says. 'I guess they would say they've got their job to do, to report to the world, but when you're trying to help people, the last thing you want is some guy standing there taking photographs, and almost tripping over you.' The paramedic Dave Weir recalls one reporter coming, uninvited, into the back of his ambulance and asking 'who I had and what his injuries were'.

Inside the hotel, 'on the fifth floor, I think', fire officer

Fred Bishop encountered a TV crew. He had to grab a cameraman to stop him walking through a door into a room which had collapsed.

'Stop!' Bishop said.

'Ah – I can see them working round the corner, I really want to get a kind of close up,' the cameraman said.

'Well, if you go through that door, the only close up you'll get is the basement.'

'How do you mean?'

'Just open the door slowly and just look.'

'Oh my goodness! I was going to step straight through there.'

'Yes – it goes all the way to the basement.'

Bishop decided he couldn't afford to spend any time looking after reporters, and ordered them to leave, sending a colleague to escort them out. 'And they did leave the building. But as soon as [the fireman] left them, they came back in again up another staircase at the back.'

Jon Buss, crime and fire reporter for Brighton's local paper, *The Argus*, was used to being woken by the phone.

> Every night, three or four calls, through the night, about fires in places like Eastbourne, Hastings, Rye, Crawley, Chichester. The fire brigade would ring me up, or the police would ring me up, and tell

me about things. All through the night. And some I used to go out on, some I didn't, I sort of made an instant decision. And when I was rung up, just around three o'clock on the 12 October, and a voice said there's been a bomb at the Grand, I sat bolt upright in bed and said, 'Fuckin' hell!' I'd never done that before, and so my wife was rather surprised at that reaction.

The biggest crime in a situation like that is to rush off by yourself, because you're going to need other people there, particularly photographers. You're going to need help. [But] I didn't even know if it was true. I just had a phone call, not from the police, not from the fire brigade. The phone call came from [a] famous freelance in Brighton, and a friend of mine.

I needed to work out what to do. Was it true? Well, too dangerous to assume it wasn't true. Calling out the cavalry and it not being true – that would have been terrible. But it was a risk I had to take.

So, before setting off, Buss phoned the picture editor and told him. He then tried the news editor's number, but, eager to get going, didn't let it ring for very long before hanging up and trying the deputy news editor. 'He answered, and I shouted down the phone at him, "There's been a bomb at the Grand, get Millsy,* get everyone. I've told photographic, I'm on my way." And then I put the phone down. That was duty done.'

Junior *Argus* reporters Kate Parkin and Jill Wells found out independently, by chance. They were living with a BBC radio reporter, who wasn't at home that night. 'His news desk had got obviously [a] really early shout. And so our phone kept ringing. And I think we probably just ignored it a couple of times, because it's in the middle of the night, obviously. And then, because it kept ringing, I got up and answered it.' The BBC man not being there, Parkin said something like 'Can I help?' or 'Is it important?' The reply was, 'Oh, yeah, a bomb's gone off at the Grand.'

'It sounds awful, doesn't it, to say you're excited,' Parkin says. '[But] I can still feel that adrenalin now. You didn't hesitate, to think. Just heard the words "bomb" and "the Grand", and we just went. You didn't even have to think about it. Yeah, it was exciting.'†

Parkin and Wells lived nearby, and got to the scene early. 'It was just silent. Complete hush. We walked right in front of the hotel, right up to it. And we were just crunching on

---

* Phil Mills was the deputy crime reporter.
† Parkin has elsewhere recalled that she actually phoned the fire brigade and her news editor before setting off.

this glass, broken glass, which was everywhere. And that's all you could hear.'

Jon Buss, who lived about four miles away, says he:

> Drove to Brighton, and I knew then that it was true because I could see the volume of police and fire brigade traffic on the road. I arrived at the scene, and of course parked the car there. There were no barriers or anything, it was still happening.
>
> Things like that, when there's huge events, they kind of... there's a hum of the electrical stuff, and the fire brigade [equipment]. And the place vibrates, the whole scene vibrates. And this was vibrating bigtime, visually and aurally and physically. It was an extraordinary sight. And there were still people wandering around with rubble on their clothes, and still people being rescued inside.
>
> In the next few hours, one by one, it was like the drawing together of the Magnificent Seven out of the gloom, with their notebooks, until we had quite a team there. And we had a little meeting. I wasn't smoking at the time, but I remember asking one of the reporters for a cigarette. 'OK, what are we going to do?' There was no news editor there, it was just us reporters, and we said 'let's just fan

out and interview everything we see that's moving.'

And that's what we did.

'We got out of the bus and literally were besieged by journalists, who came running over saying, "Who are you?", and whatever,' says Michael Colacicco, from the C13 forensics team. 'We're still not being told what we're there for.' A Sussex officer approached Colacicco.

'Are you C13?'

'Yes.'

'I hear you're coming to take over the scene.'

'What scene?'

> And we walked round the corner, and I'm now faced with what's left of the front of the Grand Hotel, all the fire engines, John Gummer and other Cabinet ministers are holding talks on the seafront.
>
> So we're having this dialogue of, 'Have you considered secondary devices? Get the area clear. You need to preserve the scene.' But the fire brigade are still looking for possible people who are still alive, you've still got people being dug out.

The rescue work was a complication, from a CSI point of view.

Bob Thorn, who was head exhibits officer for this scene, says:

Ever heard of Locard's exchange principle? This is the mantra that you have as an investigator [at] a crime scene. Locard's exchange principle is that if any two materials meet, there is an exchange of material. If I shook hands with you, you now have got some of my skin cells, I've got some of your skin cells. And that applies on every object. When you walk out of this house, you'll have some material of my carpet on your socks. That, scientifically, is very important.

But there's an adverse effect of that, and that is that, this is my bomb scene. I've got fire engines on there, I've got ambulances driving away, and they might have a vital piece of evidence stuck in the tyres. They might have brought some stuff in and it's dropped off the tyres.

The fire brigade, you can't say every time they come out, 'Let's sweep your boots, mate.' They've just got to do what they've got to do. It's horrendous for us, bearing in mind my job, because you think, the vital bit of evidence might be going out. But [there's] nothing you can do about it.

Though Thorn appreciated that the rescues had to be prioritised, he still felt 'just pure frustration. Pure frustration. It's bad enough being all ready to do a job, and you've just got to sit and wait for someone. But you're watching them wrecking the scene that I've got to interpret, that I've got to recover from.'

It was decided that Mrs Thatcher should go to Lewes Police College for the remainder of the night. She was escorted out of Brighton police station, past a crowd of reporters. She stopped to talk to them. Once she'd answered three brief questions, a protection officer said, 'I think that's enough, Prime Minister.' But she delayed a while longer.

'You hear about these atrocities, these bombs, you don't expect them to happen to you. But life must go on, as usual,' she said.

'And your conference will go on?'

'The conference will go on... The conference will go on, as usual.'[13]

Chief Constable Roger Birch arrived at John Street around this time.

> On the way there I was very worried because we'd
> had a... it was false, but a secondary threat, we
> thought there was another bomb, another attack.

> And I was desperate to get her away. And of course,
> as she came out of our police station, she stopped on
> the pavement. I just wanted to get her into the car.

'There was a lot of worry with that,' police protection
officer Les Crabb says.

> I mean, having taken all these precautions of getting
> her out, getting her into a safe house, the damn
> woman wanted to stop and have a chat. Anybody
> could have been there. Yeah, she just insisted on
> doing it, and what can you [do], apart from grabbing
> hold of her and dragging her away? Which wouldn't
> have gone down too well, would it? Especially in
> front of all the TV cameras.

Once Thatcher was away safely, Roger Birch went
upstairs.

> The first chap I saw was Geoffrey Howe. There
> were a group of people in the chief superintendent's
> office, some of whom I recognised as VIPs. Scantily
> dressed, absolute chaos. And Geoffrey Howe said,
> 'Good morning, chief constable.' I thought, 'it's not
> a particularly good morning', but, typical Geoffrey

Howe. And he said, 'Do you know the American ambassador?' who was sitting at this desk.

So there we were, in funny old clothes, shoes and God knows what. I worked out who was there, and they were immediately saying, 'Well, who is missing, who's been killed?' That was the major difficulty, knowing who was missing, who had been killed. One of the things at that time, before conference security was developed – we had no idea who was in the hotel. They might have gone out for dinners, doing other things. And so it was extraordinarily difficult to work out exactly who of the VIPs were missing or dead.

'There were masses of people in the police station, a lot of them very dusty and dirty and unhappy looking,' says Detective Inspector John Byford.

There were swarms of police staff coming in. I [went] to the assembly hall, where there were a lot of people. And there were one or two police officers there calming people down. Somebody was trying to get names and addresses and that sort of thing.

One particular minister was shouting the odds because he wanted to get back to his room to collect his personal belongings. He allegedly stayed there with Mrs Whatever-his-name-was, but of course it wasn't Mrs Such-and-such at all – what he was desperate to get was the underwear and stuff that had been left behind, when they'd all got out, ever so quickly. That's what he wanted. And, of course, he was pretty horrified when he was told to sign for this bundle of stuff. 'Are these yours, sir?'

Mark Stanford, one of the officers who was rushed from Butlin's to the scene, recalls that 'they improvised [with] you as you arrived. "Ooh, another one's here, great, another dozen blokes ready to go, you can do this, that and the other."' Stanford spent time standing guard around the scene.

[We would] make notes of vehicles that might be parked nearby. Anything on junctions, because you didn't know if it was relevant or not, but you'd make a note of what was in visual view, who was around, what shops were open. When people did turn up to open shops, what time they arrived, because if they were being spoken to later, they might have seen something days before – we didn't know it was a timing device till much later if I remember rightly, so you didn't know how far back they wanted to trace things. You knew it was going to be important in due course, so you made a note of who turned up, at what time. If people were walking dogs or doing other bits and pieces, again, their details were taken.

As well as potential witnesses, Stanford suggests:

You were looking for people who might be paying too much attention. Obviously it had been in the news, the headlines; you're going to get some people come down. [But] you're looking for people who might try and blend in, trying to see how things are going, might be relaying stuff back [to the IRA]. Anyone that you thought just might be left as a spotter.

PC Chris Cox recalls that some officers were sent to guard the multi-storey car parks near the Grand.

And they got bored, and they started arresting people. People who were walking about in a car park in Brighton. Not unusual, early hours of the morning, and they'd run away as soon as they saw a load of coppers. They arrested people for, 'suspicion of committing an arrestable offence'. Which was a way of saying, 'I'm bored here, get me to the police station.'

'We just carried on rescuing people, throughout the remainder of the night,' fire officer Fred Bishop says. Once each rescue was finished, 'we would call for silence, and actually call out, to see if anybody could hear us. And that's how we found the Tebbits.'

'Oh, who's that?' called a voice from the rubble.

'No, who's that?' Bishop asked.

'No – I asked first,' said the voice, which turned out to be Margaret Tebbit.

The Tebbits' bed, with them inside it, had fallen 'down about three floors, I think,' Bishop says.

And you can imagine, a couple of floors above [them] had all come down on top. [We] had to cut a lot of the bed away just to get to them. And they were completely buried inside the rubble. You couldn't see them initially; you could only talk to them.

Firemen began a careful process of shifting rubble, while trying not to move anything that could cause further collapse. Fire officer Steve Tomlin says it was a bit like the children's game pick-up sticks. 'You had to really look at what was there, and if you moved X, what fell down around it. And so that was what took the time, really. You couldn't just go in like a bull in a china shop. It's very methodical.'

While this was going on, the rescuers tried to keep the Tebbits talking. Bishop says:

> Somebody was saying to him, 'Oh, did you play conkers when you were a kid?' 'Yeah, I used to play conkers.' I said to the lads with me, 'Just think of anything, I don't care what it is, think of it, ask him questions, keep him talking.'
>
> Because all the time they were talking, we knew they were alive. I suppose that's to our benefit, really. I think it also encouraged them as well, to realise that we're there for them and we will do everything we can to get them out. So, yeah, it's one of the things that we've always done, just, keep them talking as long as you can, keep them conscious. It gives you incentive then as well.

Fred Bishop said to Mrs Tebbit, 'Can you tell me anything about your injury, Margaret?' As a former nurse, she realised she had some kind of spinal injury. But all she told Bishop was that her arms were cold. 'I didn't want to say any more, because I didn't want my husband to realise,' she later said.[14] Worried about Norman, Mrs Tebbit urged the rescuers to get him out first, but this was impossible because of the position they were trapped in.

When they freed Mrs Tebbit from the rubble, they covered her in a tin-foil-type 'space blanket'. 'I feel just like a chicken being wrapped up to go into the oven,' she said, according to Fred Bishop. 'And I thought, "you've been in that for three hours, you must be in terrible pain",' he says now. 'For her to come up with that, I thought, absolutely incredible.'

'And then we got to Norman, of course, and he grabbed my hand and he refused to let it go. He was frightened we'd kind of miss him.' Tebbit, who was conscious and coherent, asked after his wife. Bishop says:

> I lied to him about Margaret. I knew she was badly injured, I knew she was paralysed and her neck was broken. But [I] said to Norman, 'No, no, Margaret's fine, we've got her off to hospital, just to get checked over.' Because I didn't want him then worrying. If I'd said to him, 'Oh, she's so badly injured, she's likely to be in a wheelchair for the rest of her life, she's

broken her spine, broken her neck,' he would have worried. So I lied to him. And I said to him [later], 'You know, I lied to you. I had to, to keep your spirits going, because you'd got so many injuries yourself, I didn't want you worrying about your wife.' And he was worried about her, there's no doubt at all.

Fireman Paul Robb recalls Bishop climbing into 'a very, very small space' to complete the rescue of Norman Tebbit. 'It was only enough for him to get in, and all you could see most of the time was his feet sticking out, so if anything moved it would have come down on him. A lot of people at the time thought he was absolutely mad doing it, but he's of the opinion that's what he's there for.'

To get in, he had to remove his helmet, which earned him a telling off later. 'It's on TV, you working without a helmet. If you would have got injured that would have been your fault, you couldn't claim off the brigade.' Bishop says:

> It didn't even occur to me. All I knew was, it was in the way, it had to come off, and get in. And I had to lean in, and so, I was leaning, my stomach was kind of on his feet as I got my arms around him. 'Get off

> my bloody feet, Fred!' he shouted. And of course,
> I said to him, 'Norman, if I get off your bloody feet
> you'll fall into this bloody hole.' And, 'Aaah!' he was
> going. I went and put my hand round his back. He
> had a massive injury to his side.

Bishop's hand and leggings ended up covered in Tebbit's blood.

Carried out of the building and given to paramedic Dave Weir, the minister was put on two intravenous drips, and given some painkilling drugs, Weir recalls. 'He had quite severe injuries, to his shoulder, his ribcage, and his hip bone. They were quite horrific injuries.'

However, mentally he seemed 'absolutely sharp as a razor. I said to him, "Got any allergies to Elastoplast or anything like that?" and he said, "Yes, to bombs."' Tebbit asked how his wife was, but Weir didn't know the answer.

At the Royal Sussex County Hospital, he was assessed by Carlos Perez-Avila, who got the impression that 'he was an extremely robust character, despite the seriousness of his injuries.' Tebbit again asked after his wife. He also asked after the Prime Minister, and was told, 'She's not here, so presumably she's alright.'

'Imagine it for yourself: there are three floors of a large hotel collapsed, and still in the process of collapsing,' says deputy fire commander Peter Rodgers. 'And you've got an unknown... well, a very large number of people unaccounted for, and that is [the] number-one priority. So the instinct of the firefighters is to go to where the problem is. And yes, initially, it is pretty chaotic. But, later, as command builds up, it starts to settle down a little bit.'

DCI Graham Hill – who was part of the police response, but not at the hotel itself – seems to agree.

> When you have a scene like that, whatever plans you've got in place – and nobody will convince me any differently – you have a degree of time when there is a level of, 'God, what's happened, who's doing what?', until your plans kick in. Once your plans kick in, then that person's doing that, that person's doing that, and shortly, fairly shortly, you have a structure to what's happening.

Safely at Lewes Police College, after praying 'for some time', Mrs Thatcher actually managed to get some sleep, albeit 'fitfully'.[15] 'One's got to remember that she didn't know about the casualties,' says Robin Butler, her principal private secretary.

Butler himself slept on a bench in the day room.

Well, at least, I lay down on a bench in the day room. But I hadn't been lying there very long. It was, by this time, I suppose five in the morning, and I hadn't gone to sleep. And the telephone rang, and it was John Gummer, saying that it was much worse than we'd supposed when we'd left the hotel.

And they'd already found some people dead, and they were digging for Norman Tebbit and for [Chief Whip] John Wakeham. And he said, the television cameras have now arrived, so if you turn on your television you'll be able to watch it. So I then had to decide whether I would go and tell Mrs Thatcher immediately this, and I decided not to, and to leave it until she arrived.

She appeared at about eight o'clock, as I remember, and I said: 'It's much worse than we thought.' And I told her about the casualties, and I told her that I'd seen Norman Tebbit being brought out, badly injured, on the television, and John Wakeham, they were still trying to retrieve him.

Mrs Thatcher replied: 'Well, it's eight o'clock and the conference is due to start again at 9.30, and we must make sure that it starts on time.'

Butler, appalled, said: 'You can't be serious. There's

terrible things happened, you're not going to go on with the conference just as if nothing had happened, surely?'

'Well – this is our opportunity to show that terrorism can't defeat democracy.'

'It was her instinct,' Butler says now. 'I remember she said, "It's what they would have wanted" – they, the victims, would have wanted. And that phrase struck me, because I wasn't quite sure how she could have known.'

Keith Joseph had rushed out of the Grand Hotel after the explosion, pausing to grab his red boxers first, but not pausing to put on a suit. He was photographed standing on the seafront in pyjamas and a dressing gown and slippers. Other conference delegates were similarly short of suitable clothes.

At 7.30 a.m. a coach took people from near the Grand to the Churchill Square shopping centre. Conservative Party treasurer Lord McAlpine had arranged for the store to open early. He noted in his memoirs that he 'spread the word amongst Brighton's taxi drivers that anyone without clothes was to be brought to M&S. I would, I told them, settle the fares.' He stood outside the store, paying the taxi drivers and sending them 'back for more of our people'.[16]

A journalist who saw people queuing to be bussed to the shop says: 'If you ever want to understand how the

Conservatives always win elections, you just watch the organisation.'

'I think I was a fortunate kind of guy. I just didn't panic,' says fire officer Fred Bishop.

> Didn't matter what the circumstances was; I was lucky, I didn't panic. And the reason I say that, I can tell you this now, is that three years ago* I had a very serious accident, with serious head injuries, where I should have died.
>
> After I came out of hospital, after being unconscious for five days and in intensive care, I went out with my wife, just to go shopping. I was pushing a trolley, in the supermarket – I just couldn't stay in there, I just ran out and sat in the car, I was shaking. I was in a panic. And I thought, 'What the heck is this?' I'd never panicked in my life. And so, then I can think back, I think, I'm pushing a trolley in the supermarket, I'm panicking; I go to the Grand Hotel, it's massive collapse, with people running out, there's dust and dirt everywhere, there's people trapped. I just said, 'OK, lads, this is what we've got to do.' No panic.

---

* This interview took place in 2016.

One of the other chaps, one of the more senior officers, he came and said, 'I can't understand how you didn't panic.' I said, 'Well, there's no point panicking, you've got a job to do.' And I think I was very lucky in those circumstances that I could think clearly. I mean, I had to think clearly, because I was putting my men's lives at risk, I was putting my own life at risk, really. I thought clearly enough to think, 'Mm, yeah, the brigade always says I shouldn't do this.' So, I wasn't just thinking, 'Ah, quick, we've got to get into it.'

'I wouldn't say you were risking your life,' his colleague Paul Robb says, pointing out that their training helped them minimise danger.

But, of course, if you go into a burning building when everyone else is running the opposite direction. We had the training, so no, I don't think… you never thought of it as risking your life. It was just your job, that's what you did, probably the same as a soldier in a battle – you knew what was dangerous, and you also knew how to keep the danger to a minimum.

'It's just your job,' fire officer Steve Tomlin says. 'You sign up to save life, and on numerous occasions a firefighter will put his life at risk for a saveable life. And that's what we were doing. Unless you consider at the time that this is to be ridiculously stupid and no chance, well, you give it your best, don't you?'

'People say it's bravery and that, but I don't actually see it that way, and I don't think the men did either,' Bishop says. 'And when people say, "Oh, you're heroes" – we're not. We're just doing a job that we're paid to do, and we're trained to do those sorts of jobs.'

Bishop and his team worked at the scene from three in the morning until about 9.30 a.m. when relief crews arrived.

> To me, and I think to most of the men, you don't think of [the time], you just think, 'There's someone there to rescue.' Once you've got them – 'Ah, there's another one here.' You just carry on. Time is not of an essence. Not at any time did I think, 'Ah, this is going on and on and on – when are we going to be relieved?' That sort of thing – didn't think about that at all. It was just, I was there to do a job, I would do that job, till we got it finished.

'Adrenalin's a lovely drug, isn't it?' says Tomlin. 'And, all the time you're rescuing people, saving people's lives. That's what you sign up to do. So, adrenalin takes you on.'

'I must admit, you're on quite a high,' his colleague Keith Ring says. 'Obviously nobody likes to see people in distress and in trouble, but that's... we signed up to join the fire service to help people when that happens. And when we're able to help people like that, you get a buzz.'

'We kept going between about three o'clock in the morning and eight without any respite,' recalls David Skidmore, a surgeon who rushed to the scene after hearing the explosion. He recalls that, during those five hours, he didn't even pause to get a drink of water. 'You don't bother about that. Why would you bother about that? If you're a fit person you just get on with it, just like soldiers do in wartime.'

'I came home here and got straight in the bath, because obviously I'm absolutely covered in muck and dirt,' fire officer Fred Bishop says. 'And my wife came up to the bath, she said, 'It's the phone for you.' And it's my chief.'

'I need you back here immediately,' the chief said.

'I'm in the bath, sir.'

'Well, get out the bath and get down here now.'

When Bishop got there, he found that 'they just wanted lots of answers'.

I mean, the chief, initially he wanted answers of why I ordered the men to go into the building. Which, I said, 'No I didn't, they were all volunteers.' And then, 'What did you find, and how was this and how was that?' And just, questions [about] the whole night, as I viewed it and as I'd seen it. And I think he had a TV crew there that wanted a lot of answers as well, and the police were there wanting some answers. And I could only give them the answers that I knew.

There were a couple of answers I didn't give them, to save somebody's embarrassment, because, there was one member of our government, as [a] sub officer went into his room – 'Get out of my room!' he said. And the sub said, 'I'm sorry, but you're coming out.' The reason he was getting really angry was because he was in bed with a young lady that wasn't his wife. So he wasn't very pleased about that. But we promised that we'd keep quiet.

'One ought to say shock or something like that, but you get sort of carried away with the pace of events, and you just realise that there's a major job to do,' says Sergeant Paddy Tomkins, who got to the scene soon after the explosion.

And of course, the first thought – there were the Prime Minister and other highly protected people in there, and the general realisation that we needed to get people out as quickly as possible. One would like to say that one had a carefully considered risk assessment and thought about the stability of the building and so on, but we didn't. We just went in and started getting people out.

I asked a couple of [officers] to start cordoning off the access, so we didn't have people coming across the front of the building more than necessary. As it turned out, that was a sensible thing to do, both for safety reasons and for protecting evidence. But I can't say those were the reasons at the forefront of my mind at the time. It was just that the training of, secure the scene.

We were trying to get people away from the front of the building. But to say that we had a careful corralling of people and making sure that we got all the witness identities and so on, at that time, would be to exaggerate.

Our focus was on rescue, obviously, and safety, and stabilising the scene. I think that the implications of the debris [as potential evidence], and the fact that people are trampling around on the debris, including us, didn't really sink in until probably around 6 a.m., that sort of thing, after the initial search, rescue and stabilisation phase was over.

By this time, people had been walking across [the scene], driving vehicles across, etc., etc. I'm not saying it was a bit stable-door. It was unavoidable, in many ways, given the need to get people out. But yeah, that awareness cut in later rather than immediately. Again, coldly and clinically, one would like to think I felt differently, but I didn't.

'One is completely absorbed by the event,' Sergeant Tomkins says.

I don't know what your hobbies or distractions are, but now, in my later years, I like to go salmon fishing, and it's that sort of focus on something that excludes everything else. It's so absorbing.

Obviously salmon fishing is pleasant and going into a bombed hotel isn't, but it's an event that's so absorbing that it shuts out everything else, and you're just focused on that particular event and in that moment. I'm not putting this very elegantly or eloquently. But, there was no sense of passage of time, or really a sense of what was going on outside at any distance removed from where we were. We were just doing what we were doing, and it was that narrowing, really, of perception, to deal with those events.

I suppose the overwhelming feeling at the time was... I was going to say excitement, but that makes it sound like one's enjoying it. Not enjoying it, but there was an adrenalin rush, no two ways about it. There was an adrenalin rush, which I presume contributes to this narrowing of focus. There was a sort of sense of purpose in the whole thing, which, I wouldn't presume at all to put it on the same level of soldiers in combat or anything like that. But it is that, as I say, that focus, absorption.

'I think it was a near miss,' says No. 10 official Sir David Wolfson.

But, it's like you're driving down a motorway, and the car in front of you starts weaving, and it's obviously lost control – your first reaction is to get out of the way. Once you've got out of the way, the sense of 'I could have been bombed' disappears very quickly, because you're safe.

I think that there wasn't a special reaction to

the actual bomb, it was, 'Thank God.' And, indeed, that's what Thatcher said, 'Thank God', rather than, 'weren't we lucky?' It was a sense of 'there but for the grace of God go I – Now let's get on with whatever we're doing.'

CHAPTER TWO

WHO'S INTERFERING HERE?

'I don't think we have any bones broken,' a doctor at the Royal Sussex County Hospital said to conference organiser Harvey Thomas.

'Oh, you haven't either?' Harvey replied.

'But you're going to get a very big shock.'

'Listen, mate, I've just been blown up by a bomb, was buried for two and a half hours under ten tons of rubble, and brought here to the hospital. What bigger shock can I have than that?'

'You'll feel nauseous, you'll feel sick, you see.'

'OK, well, if that happens, I'll know what it is, I'll say, "this is shock", and I'll sit down and wait till it goes. In the meantime, let me get back to my conference, if I've got no bones broken.'

'Oh, you can't leave the hospital.'

'I can do exactly what I want, if I've got no bones broken.'

Harvey decided to discharge himself, against their advice. But he couldn't really leave until he had some clothes to leave in. His wife, Marlies, brought some down, by train. Harvey says:

> When she arrived at Brighton station with my mother – now, my mother at that time was in her late seventies, Marlies was very heavily… I mean, five days overdue in her pregnancy, so she was huge. And they were just pushed out of the way by the journalists who came off the train, to get to the taxis first. No manners at all.

'The one thing that struck me, being Latin,' Carlos Perez-Avila says:

> is that, in El Salvador, where I come from, there probably would have been hysteria and crying and yelling and, 'Ahh!' Here, the so-called stiff upper lip was amazing. There was no crying, there was no shock, everything was a matter of fact.

I remember going out to the reception room because there was an elderly lady, she had blast injuries to her ear, she couldn't hear very well, and she was peppered with pieces of, not shrapnel but, of the material of the [hotel] – bricks and things, completely brown. The water tanks had exploded, and with all the dust, all the water had come down, you see. So they were muddy.

And she was there sitting with a blanket. Because she was elderly, I went out to the minor-injuries [area], to say, 'Look, we can't see you, we're dealing with very serious injuries.' This was about four o'clock in the morning. So I went and I said, 'I'm terribly sorry but we're very busy.' She said, 'I expect so.' So I said, 'Yes, so you will be seen, but not just now – would you like a cup of tea?' And this lady looked at me and, she said, 'You know, there's nothing like a lovely cup of tea at four o'clock in the morning.'

Or a politician that came through with a stretcher, and I said, 'Hello, I'm Mr Perez, I'm the consultant in charge, how are you? What's your name?' And he said, 'Do you have a pen and paper?' And I said yes. He said, 'This is the telephone number of the switchboard, 10 Downing Street, make sure you

ring and say that I'm alright, and that they need
to put everything in action as per plans.' And of
course, the Conservative Party was already there,
but this guy, who had been trapped for god knows
how many hours, still had that loyalty for the...
It's something I've never, ever seen.

So it was surreal, it was just – nobody moaned.
There were serious, serious injuries, and nobody
really moaned or screamed. I don't know if you've
seen the picture when they're getting Norman Tebbit
out of the Grand Hotel, he has a grimace of pain.
He was very seriously injured. And yet, when he
arrived in the hospital, he was as quiet as can be,
and, 'Yes, doctor, thank you, doctor, what are you
going to do, doctor?' And he was very, very seriously
injured. So that sort of attitude, I had never seen,
never had come across that, ever.

'Brighton was full of journalists already, for the conference,'
says hospital press officer Andrew Partington. Dozens of
them went to the Royal Sussex. They were hungry for
information – 'desperate for anything'.

'The press were there before me,' his colleague Pam
Lelliott says. 'When I got there it was absolute chaos.'
Twelve journalists were waiting at the entrance to A & E,

'and there were others wandering around, inside, and in the wards. Everywhere, really.'

Rather than try to keep the press out, the hospital set up a room for them. But how could Lelliott get them to go there?

> This is not written in the major-incident plan, but it's quite simple. Bacon sandwiches. As dawn broke, or it was even before that – obviously the hospital has a 24-hour canteen – I knew that they wanted information, and they weren't getting it necessarily just wandering around on their own. And a good way to a journalist's heart is through their stomach. So, I got numerous bacon rolls, on a trolley, that was sent along to the press room, and then I went round telling the press that they were there. From that moment onwards, that became their home.

Partington says that providing a press room – and providing it closer to A & E than the major-incident plan recommended – was crucial.

> We could say to the press, you can come in, you can use this room, there are telephones here, we will make ourselves available. Basically, don't breach our

trust. Because we're doing this on the basis of trust, that you won't go running around and making a nuisance of yourselves. We'll be good to you, you play the game with us. And it worked.

I don't think we had any instances of journalists trying to get into the rest of the hospital; [they] followed our advice. And that, I think, was the single biggest thing we were able to do to manage it. Because if we'd kept them outside in the car park, all hell would have broken loose, because they would have seen everyone coming in and out, they would have been pestering people, they would have been trying to get in, they'd have been trying to find back routes into the hospital, past the police cordon, you name it. By getting them inside, they felt trusted. Made a huge, huge difference.

And we had consultants, managers, politicians, senior police officers, prepared to take that leap of faith. And I think, yeah, genuinely, it did stop them going off and trying to grab everybody in the corner saying, 'what's it like for you, what's it like for you, have you seen this, what did you see, what did you see?' Because they didn't need to, because we were... well, we were literally feeding them, which, psychologically, it was a great move. And feeding

them as much information as we could, which they
did respect.

Carlos Perez-Avila recalls noticing that Harvey Thomas
'wasn't injured, but was very talkative'.

> It was ideal that I had seen him come through,
> completely caked with mud and stark naked, and
> already very verbose. So I thought, 'Mm, that's the
> guy I need to keep the press happy.'
>
> He was quite happy to come and say that he
> saw God and that he was hanging from a lamp
> post or something, and dangling there, and how he
> felt that God had called him. Fine. So I played him,
> in the sense that it was very convenient for us to
> have somebody that knew the Conservative Party,
> knew the organisation of the conference, knew the
> politicians, and was able to say whatever. And the
> press were happy with that.

Thomas provided some great quotes: for example, that
he'd initially thought the explosion was an earthquake.
'But then I thought, no, you don't have earthquakes in
Brighton – at least not during a Tory Party conference.'[17]
He described how, from his trapped position, 'I had to

scratch and claw to keep the rubble away from my face and squirm to stay away from water cascading from a fractured pipe. At least I hope it was water.'

Harvey recalls:

> The hospital said to me, 'Well, you're basically not structurally damaged, but you look as though you're three-quarters dead, so it'll be great for the media, they'll be very pleased. Would you mind going out there and being the sacrificial lamb,' kind of thing. So I said fine. And I hadn't had a chance to wash or do anything at that point, or even clear some of the rubble out of my ears or anywhere. So I was a pretty big mess. But all I could see was this sun-gun and this guy asking questions. I did not know there were, I think, twenty-seven cameras behind him.
>
> And I didn't realise that till later in the day. An old friend of mine from Bible College in Minneapolis, who I hadn't seen for twenty-five years, who was married with her family in California, sent me a telegram, addressed to 'Harvey Thomas, care of Margaret Thatcher, Brighton, England.'
>
> So the telegram came through, and I went in to see Mother – we used to call Mrs Thatcher 'Mother'. And I went in to see her, and she said, with half the

Cabinet all there, 'Oh, Harvey, I've got a telegram here for you, shall I read it to you? It says: 'Dear Harvey, I saw you on television here in California this morning. Do you know, we've known each other twenty-five years and I've never seen you naked before? Love, Diane.'

Concerned to get Mrs Thatcher safely into the conference centre, Sussex chief constable Roger Birch had asked for her to be brought in through the back entrance. But, presumably to show how business-as-usual everything was, 'she went to the front. Typical Margaret Thatcher!' says Birch, who had been waiting for her at the rear of the building.

So we all dashed over to the front. At this stage, I thought, 'this is the end of my career.' Doom and gloom. I felt pretty low. I'd not been to bed. I felt shattered, to be truthful. A lot of pressure from the media all night. And the only thing that cheered me up, as Maggie and her top team moved through the VIP area, [Deputy Prime Minister] Willie Whitelaw said, 'Don't worry, Roger, it'll be alright.' That was tremendous, for me. When you've got that sort of responsibility, that little bit of reassurance, from somebody that matters, is quite important.

Everyone attending the conference was a potential witness. Sussex Police wanted to try to speak to as many of them as possible, while they were still in town. To this end, DCI Graham Hill went to the hospital; his colleague John Byford went to the conference centre, where he approached Health Secretary Norman Fowler, with a request.

Byford recalls telling Fowler:

> What I need to do is to get, unfortunately, the names and addresses of all of these delegates, every last one of them, to find out where they were during the night, and that sort of thing. I will set up a facility outside in the entrance with officers to see people; we want at some stage during the morning for them all to make sure that they see a police officer. If this doesn't happen, we'll be in a situation where we will have to follow it up afterwards, which is going to be much more difficult and involve people all over the country.

'You want me to say this to our delegates, do you? It'd be much easier if you said it,' Fowler said.

'You are a very well-known person. I'm a nothing as far as these people are concerned,' Byford replied.

'Alright, come with me.'

'So I went and stood on the stage beside him,' Byford says.

> [The audience] was a bit noisy, but as soon as he said
> that he'd got a police officer with him, and with an
> important announcement to make, you could have
> heard a pin drop. They were so absolutely rapt, and
> he said his few words, and then, as I say, handed
> the mic to me. I didn't have much to say.
>
> I think another good thing was that it showed
> that we, the police, were on top of it right from the
> start. Here, at this time of the morning, here is a
> detective who wants things done.

'I've never really been one for shock and trauma,' Harvey
Thomas says.

> But I was concerned about a number of things. First
> of all, I was naturally concerned about my friends
> who'd been killed, five of them, and also injured.
> But I was also concerned – who is trying to interrupt
> my conference? Because that's what conference
> organisers and producers are like. They're very
> possessive. So the first concern was for the injured
> and the dead, of course. But after that, my thought
> was: 'Oi, who's interfering here?' And I was quite

sure Mother would want to go on schedule, which she did.

So, once his wife had arrived with some clothes, Harvey set off for the conference centre.

When Mrs Thatcher saw him, she said 'My god! We thought you were dead'.[18] Harvey recalls:

> Well, see, I'd been missing, presumed dead, for about two and a half hours that morning. And they all thought I was dead. But I'm a very normal sort of character, so I don't say, 'Da-dah, here I am.' It was a question of wandering in and somebody says, 'There's Harvey, he's not dead.' It wasn't a dramatic thing. It was carrying on as routine, as far as I was concerned.
>
> I was very tired, but then you're always tired on the last day of a conference anyway. And you sort of don't think about it. This was the thing. We hadn't been clever enough to invent post-traumatic stress. In those days we just got on with it. It was a different world. We didn't have all these kind of pansy type things we have today where everybody's 'Oh-ahh'. We had a job to do, and [we] did it.

By and large you just got on with it, you didn't faff around saying, 'Oi, where's somebody who can give me sympathy?' I didn't miss a day's work, I never had that shock, it never caught up with me.

It might have been different had I had a leg amputated, or something structural like that. I only make light because I didn't get structural damage. Not in any way lacking in sympathy to those who did, because it would have been very difficult. And I don't know how I would have reacted. But when there was nothing broken – right, then you get on with it.

'The atmosphere at the conference centre was terrible,' Ann Widdecombe says.

Everybody, everybody, was asking about somebody that they couldn't find. I mean, absolutely everybody. We didn't know who was alive, who was dead, who was still under the rubble. We didn't know. And, everybody was saying: 'Have you seen so-and-so? Is so-and-so alright? So-and-so was at the Grand.' And that was the atmosphere.

Widdecombe, who had been hanging out at the Grand Hotel's bar until 'about half an hour' before the explosion, 'was looking for the people who'd been in the bar with me. And saw somebody, and one or two of them had dust inhalation, but apart from that, they were OK.'

I saw a couple, who therefore told me that everybody else had also got out. But there was an elderly lady that I was very close to. And I knew she'd been in the Grand. And it was absolutely ages before I was able to find out that she was alright, absolutely ages. And none of us knew. You weren't getting figures saying, 'five dead, and here they are.' We just knew that some people had been killed. We knew others were in hospital. It was awful.

Nobody was trying to give the impression that everything was OK. What we were saying was: 'The IRA is not going to stop us. We're going on. We have a conference, this is not going to disrupt it, that would be another victory for the IRA.' That was the attitude at the time. Nobody was pretending that everything was fine. Clearly it wasn't. People were being pulled out of the rubble all day.

There was a sense that you carried on, and you showed the IRA that you were going to carry on. But nobody said you mustn't be worried about anybody – nobody said that.

The first press conference, four hours after the bombing, had been 'a bit shaky', says Roger Birch, Sussex's chief constable,

> because there was so much demand for information. And of course, as you well know, your trade, the rumours spread. And there were a lot of rumours, which we couldn't dispel but which we guessed were probably rather wrong. So you're, all the while, having to play a fairly negative game. The major problem was how many people were killed, who are they? And we didn't really know. At least, it took some time.

One thing Birch was able to say that day, *The Argus* noted, was that 'somewhere along the line, something has gone wrong.'

'The absence of any firm information was very striking, for most of that first day,' says Simon Strachan, a senior Brighton hospitals official who helped with the Royal Sussex's press response. 'In fact, statistics which you'd think would be readily available were very hard to identify.'

His colleague Andrew Partington says:

> From memory, first thing that the hospital had to do, and we had to do, is to confirm who we'd

actually got. So at any one moment it was, "how many have we got, how serious are they, how many have been discharged?' And I can remember me and [two colleagues] literally working through this handwritten list. Because [we had] no computerised records then.

We were grabbing bits of paper and working out what was going on: 'OK, this person's come in, this person's been discharged, take 'em off the list, this person's in, this person's been treated, this person's in the operating theatre, think this one's dead, check that later, don't confirm anything till we know that next of kin have been informed.' So we got to a point mid-morning where we could say, 'Alright, this is the definitive list of who's been treated and discharged. This is who we've got currently being treated.'

The NHS has got reasonable protocols in place anyway [about giving out information]. And always did, always has done. So first of all, no information without consent. Secondly no information unless the next of kin already know it. So that kind of defines the level of detail that you can give.

But, of course, the world had seen Norman Tebbit being carried out on a stretcher, under the

TV lights, and wanted to know how he was. So, when something is already out in the public domain like that, you have to make a judgement call. The minimum would have been: 'Yes, we can confirm he's a patient right now.' 'Well, yeah, of course we bloody know he's a patient, mate, we've seen him being carried out the hotel on a stretcher! How is he?'

And, we thought, 'Yeah, fair point.' You've actually got to be realistic in situations like that. So [David Bowden, the district administrator] is in touch with the surgeon, four floors up in the operating theatre, who phones down what he's doing to Norman Tebbit, and between the hospital manager, myself, Pam, the police and the Conservative Party chairman, we agree a form of words that basically says, 'These are his injuries, he's in surgery at the moment, he's doing well, we'll let you know more when he's out and recovering', or something like that.

Scribbled down on a piece of paper, took it out to the press room. Said, 'OK, we've got an update on Norman Tebbit.' Everybody turns and looks. David Bowden reads that out. From then on, we managed to get [the situation] under control, because, having given them that information about Norman Tebbit, live, as it were, they said, 'Yeah, OK, I can see you're giving us what there is.' And then the food came out, they were really happy, they could phone up their offices, phone all the copy back, from the press room, inside the [security] cordon.

'*The Argus* always regarded itself as a little London paper really,' says its political reporter Adam Trimingham. 'And this [was] a chance to show that we could do the stuff.'

However, news editor Chris Oswick says:

Normally, as the local paper, you get the jump on the nationals. If a big story breaks in Brighton, there's a road crash or a fire, you've got people on the scene, and [the national papers] have to come down from London. This was the direct opposite, because, of course, the nationals and international press were in the Grand Hotel and around. We were in our homes around Brighton. So this was, almost uniquely, an occasion where the nationals had the start on us.

Undeterred, the team set about putting together a first edition which would be ready in time for delegates at the conference to read. 'I wouldn't describe it as frenzied, but it was certainly busy and excited,' says Oswick.

It was just – get something out, get started. I always used to talk about the Steve Davis technique. In any profession, it seems to be, if your skills are properly honed, if you know what you're doing, then in a crisis, you're just expected to go on doing the same thing time and time again, only you're doing it at a higher level, under greater intensity. But if you just go on doing what you normally do, and you can keep your nerve, you come out alright in the end.

Press officer Andrew Partington recalls:

The first edition of *The Argus* being delivered to the hospital on the Friday morning. They'd done a blinder, *The Argus*, obviously, all hands to the pump, first edition, they'd given complete reportage of everything that had happened up to that point. And it got pounced on by all the national reporters, who promptly rewrote it for all their publications.

'There were lots of stories about mystery people doing mystery things,' recalls *Argus* reporter Jon Buss.

On the night of the bomb, there was a mystery man with an afro haircut and flared trousers and some kind of bright top, and he was carrying something, and he was seen running away [from the scene]. He was public enemy number one for a while. And he was seen by somebody who told the reporter, very confidentially, that he had training in this kind of thing and he knew a bad 'un when he saw one, and this guy was a bad 'un.

And that made it into the paper the day of the bombing. And it may well have been me, but I'll try and claim it was one of my colleagues, I think, that wrote that. But there were all sorts of conspiracy theories. And, of course, immediately after it happened, no one … first of all people didn't know that it was a bomb, they thought it was maybe a missile from the sea.

Was it difficult to separate rumour from fact?

I don't remember [being] interested in separating rumour from fact at the time. You were reporting what people were saying and thinking. If you stopped to think, for instance, about the man with the funny haircut and flared trousers, you wouldn't put it in the paper, would you? But you just interviewed everything that moved and stuck it in the paper, and that's how it was for a week or two afterwards. So, I think it's probably fair to say that we were working at such a frenetic pace and we were so absorbed in what we were doing that we probably didn't care too much to separate what was ridiculous and what was rumour from what was true. But, looking back, I don't see that as being too bad. You were reporting what was going on. It was like, the internet today is a lot of rubbish, with the truth in there somewhere. And that's the same when you've got a huge story like this. And other people will report the rubbish if you don't.

We would print anything that moved, really. I'm sure there was lots of rubbish printed, I'm sure I wrote lots of front-page leads that were doubtful in their authenticity, but then that was the name of the game. I'm sure readers lapped it up.

'In a way, we were part of the story as well,' says Chris Oswick.

The telephone is king, and people were phoning anything with a Brighton address to get an angle on the story. And I remember doing an interview just after the first edition had gone off with, I think it must have been the Sydney *Morning Herald*.* They asked me, 'Is this the work of the IRA?' And, do you know, that was the first time the IRA had come into my mind. We were so busy finding out what had happened, the extent of the damage, how many casualties... We were still in the 'what happened' phase of the story, rather than who was responsible. It really hadn't occurred to me to think about the IRA at that stage.

My job was to get the reporters on the scene, telling me what had happened, what it looked like, what it felt like. And the actual cause of it and what lay behind it, right up until that time hadn't occurred to me. I have to say, I went straight out into the newsroom and went: 'Bloody hell – the IRA!' Or words to that effect.

'There's a certain busyness that envelops a hospital, a certain sort of buzz of getting on with the stuff,' hospital administrator Michael Forrer says.

It always amazes me when you have a major-incident

---

* Oswick later corrected himself – he believes it was actually an Australian radio station.

practice in a hospital, even though people are usually told it's a rehearsal so nothing dire happens, you get a whole organisation of a couple of thousand people on duty or whatever, all of a sudden attuned to a task. And all the issues about, 'Oh dear, I'm tired, I've worked X shifts this week', or 'I don't like the way so-and-so is behaving', all these things go completely out of the window – the things that any organisation has, whatever they do. And people just focus on what they've got to do. And somewhere like A & E is clearly a place where that happens.

The callout goes out for a major incident, for extra staff, but people phone in anyway, or just turn up, in those circumstances. Junior medical staff, nursing staff, the lot. Administrative staff as well, pathology staff. And I think that would have happened whether it had been a totally non-high-profile thing. I'm absolutely convinced that would have been the case.

Hospital press officer Pam Lelliott says a joke went round the hospital that for the first time ever, every doctor was there – including gynaecologists.

'The beauty of the emergency services in this country is that you cater for each and every eventuality, and the one thing that people do is, just to do their job,' Carlos Perez-Avila says.

> And that's what happened. The orthopaedic surgeon was in the resus room, he rang theatre and said, 'I'm sending Joe Bloggs, he has this and this and this and needs this doing', so the patient went to theatre, the surgeon in theatre then rang intensive care and said, 'We've just finished with Joe Bloggs, he needs a bed, I've done this and this and this.'
>
> So there was extremely good communication between all the staff. The physicians in the hospital ensured that [any patients] that needed to be in hospital were kept in hospital, the ones that didn't need to be in hospital were shipped home, with follow up appointments and... The whole thing is like a clock that ticks, and all the gears fit into this thing. Management, for instance, in the control room, do you need more beds, do you need blankets, do you need...
>
> It worked very well. So I was chuffed that it worked very well. I don't think I had a sense of pride. I did my job. As a matter of fact I was to a certain extent embarrassed about [receiving an] OBE, embarrassed in the sense that it's... in A & E,

consultants are low-key people. As a matter of fact it's quite embarrassing when you go to El Salvador and meet your university friends and they say, 'Oh, Sir Perez', and I say, 'I'm not a sir!'

I remember somebody ringing me up. They said, 'I saw you in the newspaper. Well done, you're going to be a lord.' And I said: 'You must be bloody joking! I'm just doing my job.' Because I didn't see it as a thing of great relevance.

Margaret Thatcher's conference speech had been rewritten to reflect what had happened. She delivered it without an autocue, as 'the press had sometimes called her the sincerity machine, and I didn't want any possibility of them being rude about the sincerity machine on the bomb day, when five people had been killed,' Harvey Thomas says.

Mrs Thatcher's speech, or perhaps merely her presence and her manner, received an almost eight-minute standing ovation.[19] The key passage denounced the bombing as:

an attempt not only to disrupt and terminate our conference; it was an attempt to cripple Her Majesty's democratically elected government. That is the scale of the outrage in which we have all shared, and the fact we are gathered here now – shocked, but composed and determined – is a sign not only that this attack has failed, but that all attempts to destroy democracy by terrorism will fail.[20]

Charles Moore, Thatcher's authorised biographer, says:

She had drafted a more partisan version before the bomb. Which she then altered because of the bomb, because it obviously wasn't appropriate to attack Labour in that context, on that day. But she did actually keep in, very strongly really, the criticism of extremists. And she meant – and made clear that she meant – Scargill and his people, as well as the IRA. So she characterised what was going on as a confrontation between democracy and extremism. She did link IRA extremism and Scargill extremism, and she meant to do that.

She'd only slept for an hour or something in her clothes, but she looked incredibly neat and she was very energetic. It was a most bravura performance, and that was very important in her reputation, and still is, actually. And it makes very good television, if you look at the clips now. I also think that it helped her with the miners' strike, in the sense that, what people slightly forget is that the miners' strike was going rather badly for her before the bomb. It had been a very difficult period, for a number of reasons, and people were rather sick of her behaviour about it. There was a school of thought, people like the Archbishop of Canterbury were saying, 'You're being too tough, you're being too nasty.' And that was getting a bit of traction.

And, of course, Scargill was always trying to get going the idea that she was refusing perfectly good deals, which actually wasn't the case, but that was always there, that idea. So I think the bomb helped her against all that and it increased her popularity in the polls, and it increased her prestige, and it gave a stronger sense of her power. And, though in a way it showed vulnerability, it did give a stronger sense of her power. And I think it helped her fight the miners' strike, actually. And it was really... I would say that in the course of, October and perhaps November – I forget the exact dates – it became absolutely clear that Scargill couldn't win the miners' strike.

Leading fireman Steve Tomlin and his crew were back at the scene late afternoon, for a shift which essentially involved trying to recover bodies. 'That's when the stress comes in,' he says.

Because you've gone past the, in your mind, 'If I work hard I'm going to rescue somebody'. Now, tragically, the incident's probably, twelve, fifteen hours down the road, and the chances of survival diminish. You've still got your hope, but it doesn't always make it easy, does it?

That Sunday, Mrs Thatcher went to church. 'She was reported by others who attended the service to be pale and visibly upset,' *The Times* noted. On the Monday, in a TV interview, she said:

The sun was just coming through the stained glass windows and falling on some flowers right across the church, and it just occurred to me that this was the day I was meant not to see, and then all of a sudden, I thought: 'There are some of my dearest friends who are not seeing this day!' And had you been able to see the previous Sunday what would happen during the coming week, you could not have endured it, you just could not have endured it.[21]

The interviewer asked how Mrs Thatcher lived with 'the constant threat of violence'. She replied: 'Well you just get on with your daily work, and that is pretty absorbing.'

'I think she behaved entirely in character' at the conference, Charles Moore says.

> She would always think, 'I'm the Prime Minister, there's been an attempt to overthrow me and the government, and we're at our party conference, it's absolutely obvious that we go on as much as possible as before in order to show that we mean business and they are not going to win.' I think that was completely instinctive with her, and very much in character. And, whatever personal fears and upset she may have had, she locked up, and they came out later when she went to Chequers at the weekend, and famously said, afterwards: 'This was the day I was not meant to see.'
>
> One of the things that people slightly misunderstand about Mrs Thatcher is, because she's very… can be very stern and determined, they think [that] she's quite cold and doesn't really have any normal human reactions. But that's not true; she's a very passionate person. Very passionate. But the passion was very much engaged, in her mind, in doing her job. That's what she put her passion into. So there wouldn't be this great contrast between the private feeling and the public-policy feeling; the two would march together.

She's wartime generation. So you're certainly
trained not to go on about your suffering and things,
because you remember the sufferings of millions of
people going on all round you. So nobody's going
to listen to your whining, when you're in a mass
situation like that, in the Second World War. But it
doesn't mean she's not emotional. As I said before,
she was a very emotional person. But she wanted
to deal with that by getting on with things, rather
than by emoting all over the place in public. But she
was passionate and her expressions were passionate
on this subject, both about the wickedness of the
terrorists and of the little thing about – well, not
so little – 'this was the day I was not meant to see',
and so on.

Thatcher hadn't stuck around to mingle with the audience
after her speech; she wanted to get to the Royal Sussex.[22]
'If you've got the Prime Minister coming to visit a hospital, that's a big deal anyway,' says press officer Andrew
Partington. 'When you've got that overlaying everything
else that's going on, it's like, "Alright, well, we're going to
have to deal with it." It was almost so big that it wasn't
worth thinking about.'

Thatcher insisted on seeing all the bomb victims who

were still there. She was taken round the wards by Julia Cumberlege, chair of Brighton Health Authority. At one point Cumberlege said: 'Now we're going into the intensive care, and you realise it's quite brutal.'

'Of course!' Thatcher said.

'Then when we went in, and she went to people's bedsides, and talked to them, and then quite briskly we went round the wards,' Cumberlege says.

> She was very much the Prime Minister, and, certainly in front of her colleagues and friends, she was very authoritative – she usually was. It was when she saw the [injured] policeman that she burst into tears. I think it was the thought that, here was this man, having nothing to do with the Conservative Party, doing his duty, in front of the Grand Hotel. And was caught in the blast.

'To me what was absolutely remarkable, absolutely remarkable, is her composure,' says Carlos Perez-Avila, who joined them for tea. 'I was shattered by this time; it was five o'clock, or four o'clock. I was absolutely knackered, and I hadn't slept at all – the tension, the adrenalin, and everything.'

'Well done, it all went very smoothly,' Carlos recalls Mrs Thatcher saying.

'Yes, ma'am.'

'So, you come from El Salvador?'

'Yes, indeed.'

'You know, President Duarte, he's a good guy. I met him two years ago, three years ago,' she said. This impressed Carlos.

Who, having not slept at all, being blown to bits, taken by car, police car, to Sussex police station in Lewes, told to go to Downing Street, refused to go to Downing Street, rewrites a speech, delivers a speech, doesn't sleep a wink and is perfectly coiffured, and still at five o'clock, four o'clock, remembers the bloody President of El Salvador?

CHAPTER THREE

WORKING FLAT ON YOUR BACK

'When I regained consciousness,' says Norman Tebbit, the badly injured Trade and Industry Secretary, 'I obviously didn't know initially where I was, or couldn't recollect what had happened – how did I finish up here? But there was a nurse sitting beside the bed, waiting for me to recover consciousness, so then I was told, and recollected what had happened.'

When his children arrived to see him,

I wasn't terribly wide awake. I'd had the first

emergency operations to stabilise my condition, and I was obviously taking, or being given, a lot of painkillers, so I was not really terribly clear about who was there and whether they were real, or whether I was hallucinating, dreaming or what. I don't know if you've ever had a serious amount of anaesthetic and that, but you're not quite yourself for a bit.

'Secretary of State, what happened to your hair?' asked Tebbit's principal private secretary, Callum McCarthy, when he visited. The minister's hair was sticking up.

'Oh, well, that was when I was electrocuted.'

'Just imagine this,' McCarthy says now.

This is a man who was in bed next to his wife, surrounded by rubble, knowing his wife is badly hurt, no longer in contact with her, with cold water running down through it, and every so often there's an electric shock that goes through the water. Not a good experience. He told me in a matter-of-fact way this terrible story.

'He looked pretty rough, as you'd expect,' says Ruth Thompson, Tebbit's private secretary.

Lots of cuts and bruises around his face and hands. That's all we could see really. He was perfectly conscious and compos mentis, but he was talking like someone who'd had a profound shock, not surprisingly.

And we didn't stay very long, we just went and said, 'here we are.' And then we started to think about how to put things back together again. And nobody quite knew, because they didn't know how long he was going to be in hospital, anywhere, let alone in Brighton. And we knew, by that point, that Margaret Tebbit had been really badly injured.

Yes, he was very matter-of-fact, as you would expect of him. He was always a very phlegmatic individual. The impression I came away with was that he wants us to know that he's quite glad to have seen us, and that we're to go away and tell people that he's still alive and kicking.

'On the Saturday night,' hospital press officer Andrew Partington says,

a freelance journalist in Brighton sold a story to *The Observer*, based on a conversation he'd had with a nurse going off duty. Who said that Margaret

Tebbit was paralysed. So, about ten o'clock on the Saturday night, we get a phone call, from *The Observer*, saying we need a line from the hospital to confirm this. Shit.

OK, what do we do now? Let's deal with it. There's no point getting angry about it, berating someone, holding an inquest on it – it's out there. How are we going to manage it? That's what we had to do.

The rules say, strictly, we shouldn't have said anything. But, knowing that the story was out there, it was only going to get worse. Once *The Observer* had run it, everyone would be phoning up. The rumour mill would have gone into overdrive.

And other people coming out of that hospital would have said things, either other visitors, other politicians, people who knew the Tebbits. It would have just spiralled out of control. So we knew the only thing that we could do would be to go as far as we possibly could.

As Partington recalls it – 'don't take this as gospel' – Mrs Tebbit's situation was that:

there was swelling on the spinal cord, and until

the swelling went down, you wouldn't know how lasting the damage would be. And that was the true clinical situation at that time. And that was all we said. 'We can't tell at the moment, nobody can tell, when the swelling goes down then doctors will be able to give a more formal assessment.'

And that was what we ended up having to put out. As far as I can recall, the Tory Party office checked that out with the Tebbits. But, of course, that then became the big human-interest story. And as soon as *The Observer* printed this on the Sunday morning, then of course everyone else, for the Monday, was still on it and asking questions, coming back to us.

This was the only leak, as Partington remembers it.

We had actually said to the staff, 'Look, be really, really careful that all journalistic inquiries go through the press office.' And I think the hospital was so shocked by the enormity of what happened that everyone was playing ball. I think it was simply that this guy had caught someone going off duty. Journalists have a habit of setting up a conversation. And, that came out, bingo.

'By the Monday after the bomb, my private secretary had set up a temporary ministerial office at the hospital,' Norman Tebbit says. There was no discussion about whether such an unusual arrangement was possible, 'because the Prime Minister said it was possible. So did I.'

'I don't think our assumption would ever be that Norman would give up,' says his private secretary Andrew Lansley.

> The only question was: how badly injured was he? I think quite soon when I saw him – Callum may have given you the same impression – we were clear, and he was clear, that his faculties were absolutely OK and he was going to carry on. What we did, of course, quite soon thereafter, was set up an arrangement so actually the day-to-day business could be handled, and we could work with him on making sure that the only things he had to bother about were the things he really wanted to bother about.
>
> I think he was pretty much engaged, within days, literally, within several days of the bombing. Not that he expected to see all the paperwork, by any means, but he did expect [his senior civil servants] to be coming and saying: 'This is what's going on.

Do you have a view about this? Because we can make sure that your view is reflected into that.' Which is... you couldn't characterise it as, 'he's not going to be back in Parliament or Cabinet till Christmas, therefore he wasn't taking responsibility for his department until Christmas.' On the contrary, he wasn't being expected to do the physical things that were difficult, but the mental stuff he could do, and he did.

When Tebbit 'started feeling a bit better, we used to go up and have a chat,' says Sussex Police protection officer Brian Etheridge.

I think his main concern was his wife. When you think, she had really nothing to do with it, her husband was in the Cabinet, but she was there because there's a conference, week by the seaside, and she'd been injured, badly. He was very angry. We didn't speak a lot about it, because normally he wanted to talk about anything other than the bomb.

One of Etheridge's roles was 'to keep all the nosey people away. Which included journalists, hangers on... It's amazing, it's like a magnet, you get somebody like that and you get, "Oh, I'm Mr Tebbit's so-and-so". Basically you just told them to bugger off.'

One of the hospital's consultants 'was very regimental' about making sure visitors didn't tire the minister out, 'because he was quite weak,' Etheridge says. 'He was being fed through tubes and things.'

When a journalist was allowed in to interview him, Tebbit said:

> I have got several broken ribs. I am sure somebody
> knows how many, but I haven't bothered to count.
> I have got a deep cut on my left side. It is a bit
> slow to heal, because you cannot just bandage it up.
> I simply have to sit here and ooze. But overall I am
> not in too much pain.[23]

Tebbit concealed the extent of his own injuries[24] so as not to 'give any satisfaction to those who had committed the bombing,' he explains. 'Nor any of my, really, of my colleagues or my opponents. I didn't want them to have any doubts that I was going to be back on song, as I had been before.'

Margaret Thatcher was clear that his job was waiting for him whenever he was ready to resume it full time, Tebbit recalls. Though 'obviously she would have had in her mind – she must have done – the thought, "Is Norman going to make it? Is he going to recover?"'

> Apart from anything else, I was bound to have doubts about how long the Prime Minister was going to leave one of the key departments running in this sort of way, that wasn't totally satisfactory, obviously. I think there's now about four departments covering the same scope as the Department of Trade and Industry did in those days. It did cover a pretty wide waterfront. And how long could she have a Secretary of State who wasn't really carrying a full load of Cabinet work?

'That'll teach you for sitting up with a blonde at ten to three in the morning,' Gillian Butler had said to her husband, Thatcher's principal private secretary, when he got home. Then, that weekend, the Butlers went sailing on a friend's boat. 'It just shows, there weren't great panic decisions to be taken immediately afterwards,' Robin Butler says. 'Life really continued as normal on the Monday morning.'

The backbench MP John Powley says:

> The authorities, the government, the whips, all…
> I'm not saying they tried to pretend it didn't happen,

> because obviously it clearly, it did happen. But they
> were not going to allow events like that to dictate to
> [them]. There was this British stoicism, as I referred
> to it at the time; that we were going to carry on,
> business as usual, or as near usual as we possibly
> could have.

'I think the only effect was, slightly what I would call the "stable-door syndrome",' junior minister Geoffrey Pattie says. 'In the sense that lots of people were looking under their cars, who really said before, "Well, I might do it every other day", or something. I think that was the only discernible thing that I noticed.'

'During the first three days, journalists were at the hospital round the clock. They missed nothing,' according to a book on health service PR.[25] The two press officers were striving 'to feed the beast', in Andrew Partington's words, offering as much information as they could, as regularly as they could, and allowing journalists to interview patients when appropriate.

'The whole three days we ran that press office it was an adrenalin fest. It really was,' says Partington.

> And there was no time to relax, there was no
> downtime. It was work and sleep – that was it.

It was high-adrenalin, high-wire stuff, all the way through, because you never quite knew what was going to happen next. It took us most of the first day, certainly the first morning, to try and get on the front foot.

I think once we'd got through the first half day, we'd corralled the press in the press room and they didn't play silly buggers with us, everyone just relaxed a little bit, not to the stage where we could completely relax, but we could see it was working.

Yeah, it was exciting. It was a high-wire act. I think we all knew that if you didn't look down it was going to be OK. None of us had done anything this big before, and I don't think there's been anything quite as big since. So the pressure to get it right was enormous.

You're excited, you're terrified it's going to go wrong, you're buoyed up by the fact nothing's gone spectacularly wrong yet. I don't like saying I enjoyed it, because you shouldn't enjoy something like that. But there's a sense of professional pride, if you like, that you're doing as well as anyone could be expected to do given that situation, and that we were getting on to the front foot.

'We had a message fairly early on' hospital administrator Michael Forrer says, 'about [the] need for an awareness of the investigation that would follow, the forensics, which involved keeping clothes and materials, anything that came in with patients, so that they could be subject to an examination, consequently.'

'In every A & E department in the country,' Carlos Perez-Avila says,

> your local police force is there with you. So if you have a drunk driver, they will come in and ask, 'Is it alright for me to breathalyse Joe Bloggs?' And you say yes or no. So you know them and they know you and there is always a very good relationship, and that relationship is unobtrusive. For instance, we knew that they wanted all the clothes of the patients. The police have these brown bags, which are lined with plastic inside, and every item is put in that brown bag, and signed, and there's a nurse who does that. So if you cut somebody's nightie or clothes or whatever, that goes in the bag and is, 'Joe Bloggs's shirt, pyjama shirt', 'Joe Bloggs's slippers'.
>
> Because that's used for DNA and fingerprinting, etc. And there's a police officer, very unobtrusive,

whilst you're working, obviously [you have] to undress the patient. So at that point in time everything is passed to this police officer, who tags it, and whose duty is to follow what's in police jargon called the line of evidence. He must ensure that he saw when you undressed the patient, and that that was indeed the... because if not, that's inadmissible in court. That's the sort of thing that went through without any problem whatsoever.

It was 'absolutely' considered possible that the IRA might attempt a follow-up attack on the Royal Sussex hospital, says PC Chris Cox, who spent some time on guard there. 'As far as we were concerned, they were coming. In what form, nobody's quite sure.'

'We borrowed a machine from Gatwick Airport,' says hospital manager Michael Forrer.

That was rushed down, our medical photographer worked non-stop, and we produced security cards for everyone, we had police on every entrance to the tower block there. Twenty-four hours a day. By and large, that went OK. I'm aware of two members of staff who felt we were turning the hospital into a bit of a fortress. But I think we were, to some extent.

Simon Strachan recalls:

> an anaesthetist – I think it was an anaesthetist – who
> was a pretty left-wing guy. I remember he always
> used to have the *Racing Post* with him, not that
> that was relevant. But he was always bucking at
> authority and being a bit of a rebel. And he refused
> to show his identity, because this was kowtowing
> to the establishment, and ducked underneath the
> police security guard. And he was rapidly tackled
> to the ground.

'I remember the police being concerned at one stage,'
Michael Forrer says,

> that there weren't too many flowers in the windows,
> so [Norman Tebbit's] room could not be pinpointed
> externally. I think – again, memory is a terrible thing
> – but I think one of the police said 'in case of aerial
> attack'. So the window could not be spotted. So any
> excessive flowers and things were removed. I heard
> those words, and I thought 'is this… this is real, they
> are really concerned about that possibility'.

David Bowden, the district administrator for Brighton's

hospitals, hadn't initially believed that the IRA might actually attack a hospital. But, the weekend just after the bombing, he'd changed his mind. He had a worrying phone conversation with a Royal Sussex receptionist.

'Mr Bowden, I have to tell you that I've just received a call from someone with an Irish accent to say that there's been a bomb planted in a hospital in Brighton.'

'Which hospital?'

'That's all that was said. I tried to get further information but then the person rang off.'

'Now – what was I to do?' Bowden says.

This was probably about eight o'clock, eight-thirty, on a Saturday evening, and there were ten hospitals in Brighton, and it could have been in any one of them.

And what I did was to call out all of the managers concerned, and tell them, and tell them to treat this with a great level of confidence – because that could have caused absolute panic, if everybody got to know about it. The press were not informed at that time.

And I said, 'I want you out, and get as many of your staff out as possible, to check through, that there isn't [a bomb].' Now – can you imagine? Have you been to the Royal Sussex County Hospital? Well, can you imagine checking through every single department at the Royal Sussex County Hospital? This took all night. And not just that, but also at Brighton General Hospital, Hove General Hospital, the Sussex Eye Hospital, the ENT hospital, and other hospitals too.

We couldn't take a chance. If I'd have done nothing, and something had have happened, well, I'd have been castigated, and rightly so. But that was a huge effort. And what did we find? We found nothing, in terms of a bomb. It was a hoax.

Royal Sussex manager Michael Forrer recalls the hospital receiving several bomb-hoax calls.

Some were very general, some were more specific. Usually these things are filtered by somebody who knows how to distinguish. But certainly some were taken seriously by the police and us. So, on some occasions we searched the whole building, the whole site. Now, I'm sure that couldn't have been done 100 per cent, because it is an absolutely huge task. In the middle of the night, or at various times. It caused a tremendous amount of disruption and distraction.

On one occasion a package was left – a hold-all, I think it was – in a ward, in reception. The receptionist hadn't spotted who'd left it. There had to be a decision on whether to evacuate the ward. There were people seriously ill in that ward. We partially evacuated the ward. Staff knew what was going on; anyone who didn't want to stay was sort of free to go – I don't know what would have happened if no one had volunteered to stay. So [some] staff went off with those patients who left the ward. Police were involved. I stayed on the ward. We kept as far away from the package as we could. The bomb squad was called.

I'm sure the same sort of thoughts went through everybody's mind. I remember thinking of my children at that time. Anyway, the good news is it turned out to be a member of staff's squash kit. I think it was X-rayed by the bomb squad. But, in that context, it was a very, very tense moment.

'It seemed to get the nutters going, the explosion,' says PC Chris Cox.

And there were hoax bomb calls for the rest of the day. There were just loads and loads of these calls, in the first day or two. And we treated them seriously. I did. But there was a serious shortage of manpower to do those things, because everybody was concentrating, almost exclusively, on the bomb site.

'You're inundated with hoax calls,' says Sussex Police search-dog handler Leslie Jeavons. 'And, do you ignore them? You've got to deal with them. And I was being sent left, right, all over the place. I didn't have a rest day for seven weeks, had to work every day off. For six months I was just rushed off my... going from here to there, all sorts of jobs.'

Various cases were reported in the newspapers: a suspicious package, found at the Royal Albion Hotel, which turned out to be a hairdryer. Three suspicious packages elsewhere in Brighton, blown up by the bomb squad, which contained 'groceries', 'papers and a torch', and 'a biscuit tin filled with eggs and flour'. And the young man who phoned in about a bomb at Churchill Square shopping centre, which police took seriously till he phoned again to say it was a nuclear bomb.[26]

'They decided pretty quickly that there were a number of suitable mortar-base-plate sites around Brighton,' PC Chris Cox says.

And all sorts of people were sent to hunt these out, where you could sit a mortar-base plate, because that was the thing of the Irish at the time. And that their next target was going to be the police station.

So we had to guard the police station twenty-four hours a day, against an attack by the IRA with mortars. Not sure what I was going to do about a mortar. But there were, I think, six positions around the police station, round the outside, where, twenty-four hours a day, someone stood. And I did that for ages, ages and ages. It seemed to go on for months, and it was all twelve-hour shifts.

For the first day or two days, it's quite exciting, and then you start to think it's boring. And then, it's mind-numbingly boring. Especially round about three o'clock in the morning. So you take a good book, basically. Yeah, after a few days you figure out, it's not going to happen. But hey, they're still paying overtime.

'The first days, the first week, was just a question of doing what *The Argus* then did very well, which was covering every inch of the story, asking every question, using all the local contacts and everything,' says crime reporter Jon Buss.

So it was just a question of a massive amount of pages, throwing pages and pages at the story, and covering it as fully as we could. We interviewed everything that moved – that's how we approached it. We were fierce news gatherers. We didn't need too much guidance.

I was thirty-three, I knew my job inside out, I had good contacts, I would work twelve hours a day if I had to. I'd be up at three o'clock in the morning, five o'clock in the morning, covering fires and things. They let me get on with it. And there were others, too, who were ambitious, hungry, angry hacks. The news editor, Chris Oswick, was a far more educated, clever person than us, but he let the dogs of war get on with it, and we just gnawed away.

'There was undoubtedly a competitive element among reporters, and quite right, there should have been,' Chris Oswick says.

There were a small number of very talented reporters, and a large number of enthusiastic young reporters just wanting to get in on the story. But there was also a need to channel that enthusiasm, and make sure that other needs were met as well.

Starting actually nine o'clock on the day the bomb went off, [some] reporters would have been doing something other than looking into the bombing. Someone had to do all of the routine jobs, theatre reviews and... I can't remember if it was a reporter's job to gather the bingo numbers from the national newspapers. Because bingo was a big thing at that time, and one of the jobs for the first edition was to make sure that you took the bingo winners from all the national newspapers and typed them up so people could read them in *The Argus* without having to buy every national newspaper. So someone would have had to do the bingo numbers.

There was certainly an element throughout of reining in reporters, and saying, 'Yes, OK, that's the Grand Hotel bombing, but there's still the local crown court, the local borough council meeting that needs covering, there's still the general run of news.'

Kate Parkin recalls that one of her colleagues was 'very bitter because she had to go to Lewes Crown Court'.

'About two weeks after the bomb, I got an invoice from the Grand Hotel, Brighton, with a bill for that night,' conference organiser Harvey Thomas says. 'And I wrote back and said to them, "Would you mind giving me half a night's discount, because the room didn't exist after 3 a.m.?" They did cancel it, in fairness.'

After a fortnight at the Royal Sussex, the Tebbits were transferred to Stoke Mandeville Hospital, so that Margaret could be treated at their spinal-injuries unit. The helicopter journey from Brighton was planned in secret, as 'we wanted a clear run, basically,' Royal Sussex administrator Michael Forrer says.

> For all sorts of reasons. One, we knew both of them were seriously ill and we just wanted to give them a clear route out. But I think security was a major concern.
>
> [I] met with representatives of the RAF the night before, and we planned things by the minute, for her departure, and his departure, to get to the same helicopter, their possessions, everything.

Rather than using the normal helicopter-landing site, Forrer visited the headmaster of a nearby school, and got permission to use their playing field.

Norman Tebbit recalls: 'At the due time the ambulances and police cars were all drawn up, in front of the hospital, whilst we left from the back of the hospital, to go to the school playing field.' He had wanted to walk the short distance from the Royal Sussex to the field, but as an ex-RAF man,

> [I was] overruled by a female wing commander who pulled rank on me, and insisted that I would go on the stretcher. Which I didn't want to do, because I thought, the sooner I was seen to be able to walk, the better. And, so I resented that very much, but she insisted, and I eventually said, 'Well, alright. I was only a flying officer, you're a wing commander, so I'll let you pull rank.'

'I remember vividly spending time in Stoke Mandeville,' says Ruth Thompson, private secretary to Norman Tebbit. 'We had a sort of rota, there were four of us.* Basically, we decided very early on that there would be somebody there at all times, and various communication, or bits of communication, would take place.'

'We just spent a lot of time kind of sitting and chatting,' private secretary Andrew Lansley says.

> With the three of us [private secretaries], there was a

---

* This was the three private secretaries and the diary secretary.

constant process by which we were coming back to London, sitting in on meetings, taking notes, acting as his eyes and ears, coming back to him, obviously kind of telling him what was going on, what was being discussed, and so on.

I seem to remember quite a lot of it was very, very focused on keeping him up to speed on work, because actually from his point of view that was good therapy. Because otherwise he would just dwell on Margaret's injuries, and that wasn't going to help him at all, frankly.

Tebbit says:

I think without having something to do, one would have tended to have become introspective, and would have tended to think too much about my own injuries, and more particularly my wife's injuries, because it gradually became very clear that she was not going to make much recovery. And so I had to think through how we would have to manage that, which was quite complicated.

'It was as if he felt that he was partly responsible,' Ruth Thompson says.

He'd gone into public life; she hadn't married him in order to go into public life, and look what had happened to her. And so there was, he was aware of that. Was he feeling guilty about it? I don't know. He wouldn't have used the word. Did he feel shattered by it? I think he probably did.

There was something about their marriage which seemed to me to be extremely interdependent. He depended on her a lot, just as she depended on him a lot, and the change of that relationship and his realisation that that was going to be a lifetime change.

Yeah, you got a sense of that. He didn't talk about it a lot, but every now and then he would say things that certainly make you stop and think, and make you realise what he was thinking about. Did he seem to be on the edge of anything? No. Basically, it was a kind of – 'this has happened, we've got to find a way of dealing with it.'

Andrew Lansley had visited Tebbit in Brighton, soon after the bombing, with 'a particular objective, which was that I would be seen [by the press],' Lansley recalls. 'I was on the news carrying a red box in for Norman Tebbit, the purpose of which was to say: "He's alright, and he's still in charge.'' The red box, however, just contained get-well-soon cards.

Once Tebbit was at Stoke Mandeville, 'we did an access piece, for the BBC, I think,' Lansley says.

> So they could see that we were working here, and that papers were coming in and going out. We had a little in-tray, on which we put 'Back to London'. They loved that, and they put a big picture of that on the news, of Norman Tebbit's back-to-London tray, with material going back out. So we were very fixed on constantly reminding them that stuff was coming and going.

'After Norman was moved to Stoke Mandeville, he had a quite serious operation,' says his principal private secretary, Callum McCarthy.

> Because one of the things that happened was that some brick had gouged out a great chunk of flesh out of his thigh, which, if it happened to you or me and nothing else had happened, we would have been laid up in hospital for two to three weeks. So, yeah, he'd had a physical ordeal of the sort that none of us should ever have. That takes some recovering from.

Tebbit had to have part of his pelvis removed, a skin graft, and another skin graft when the initial one didn't work properly. He admits this was 'annoying', but denies it stopped him working. 'It's not only whores that work flat on their back, you know.'

'Are you normally fit and healthy?' a surgeon at Stoke Mandeville asked Norman Tebbit.

'Healthy, yes; fit, no.'

'What exercise do you take?'

'I have never knowingly taken gratuitous exercise in my life.'

'Oh dear. Do you smoke?'

'No.'

'Oh, that's better. Do you drink?'

'Yes.'

'What do you drink?'

'Mostly red wine and whisky.'

'Ah. Well, the food here is bloody awful, and I want you to put on some weight, because you obviously weren't carrying much excess weight, and now you're as skinny as hell. So I want you to eat as much of the food as you can, and to help you in that process I'll send in a crate of red wine.'

'For practical purposes he was never absent,' says Sir Brian Hayes, joint permanent secretary at Tebbit's department.

I mean, very quickly after the bomb he was seeing the papers. His brain wasn't injured, and it was working as it always did – very effectively. It just goes to show that a department can carry on in almost any circumstances. Of course, that's what it's there for. I think, just as Norman coped very, very well with the worst of it, we all coped reasonably well. It's surprising how well it worked, really.

Ruth Thompson says:

I think what would have been noticeable for civil servants who were used to meeting him would be that they weren't getting very many meetings with him. Most of the stuff was done at second hand, through the office. And that would have been noticeable. But because we were in shifts with him, it didn't feel like he wasn't there.

On 3 December, an unnamed official was quoted in the *Financial Times*: 'He's not here – but on the other hand, he's around, if you know what I mean. And from time to time, he makes his presence felt.' Another anonymous source told the paper:

You're sitting there enjoying the freedom of having the boss away… then you look through your in-tray and you find a brief missive saying: 'Hope you're not spending too much of my money while I'm away.' You wonder what on earth it is. And then you see that it's signed Tebbit.

'I think it's important to keep remembering that, I don't think any of us expected, on whatever day it was in October, that [Tebbit] would be away for so long,' says Ruth Thompson.

I think at the beginning we thought, 'Oh, he'll be back really quite soon.' A fortnight was talked about, things like that. And then that didn't look very realistic, because his injuries were found to be rather worse than people had thought. Then he had to have skin grafts and things like that. So it played itself out gradually. And then, once the elapsed time had elapsed, people were kind of used to the arrangement. And they didn't like it. No civil servant likes not to see the minister, and eyeball the minister, about difficult decisions. But nobody could complain. It's palpably not his fault that he couldn't see them.

For Geoffrey Pattie, junior minister at the DTI, the situation felt basically normal, though 'probably a bit more vicarious'. More of the communication was done by memos sent back and forth.

'If Norman had been alright,' he says,

> what would have been happening is that we would have been having more of those discussions face to face. Because Callum would ring up and say, 'Secretary of State is wondering if you could meet at twelve o'clock to discuss the XYZ project', and we'd all look at our diaries and try and get there. Well, that wasn't an option.
>
> And, I mean, it's a huge credit to Callum that it was all as good as it was. Because you felt you were almost dealing with the Secretary of State. It's simply that, you'll know what I mean by interactive, if you haven't got the interactive element, if you're actually doing a sort of slow ping-pong game really, where Callum says, 'Secretary of State thinks this', and then you say, 'Well, I'm not sure he's totally right because if you go back, you'll find that…' I mean that can take a day and a half, whereas it could have been sharply argued out in ten minutes.
>
> Whereas you would have almost put your head

round the door, in the past, and said, 'Do you think we ought to do this?' If you can't do that, you're then in a situation where you're having to slightly codify your thoughts, put down paragraphs and things. It's got a different rhythm to it. It's the difference between dealing with somebody who you're not seeing very often but who you know well and like, through an intermediary, or talking to them face to face.

Around the time of the bombing, the DTI's key piece of business was the privatisation of BT. 'It had to be taken through on the schedule that we'd set,' Norman Tebbit says. The key remaining decisions, about the pricing and allocation of shares, couldn't be postponed.

Tebbit's private secretary, Andrew Lansley, has kept a notebook from 1984, which contains a page of numbers and sums relating to the allocation of shares. 'The point is, he was not just saying in general terms. I'm writing all this stuff down because I'm showing him, because he's actually interested in the numbers and wants to actually work it out, so he's physically doing it.'

Tebbit recalls that he 'actually agreed the price for the float, with Nigel Lawson, who was chancellor, from my bed. So I was obviously, by the end of October, very much back in the driving seat again.'

At the first post-bomb Cabinet meeting on Thursday
18 October, there had been surprisingly little discussion
of what had happened in Brighton. The Cabinet had
expressed their 'deep sympathy' for the bereaved and the
injured, particularly Norman Tebbit and the Chief Whip,
John Wakeham. And they talked about the need for tighter
security. But they'd also talked about upcoming business
in the House of Commons, tensions between Iran and
Iraq, the situation in South Africa, Mrs Thatcher's recent
discussions with Jacques Delors, Britain's EU rebate, the
European Development Fund, the value of the pound,
and – in some detail – the miners' strike.

The bombing appears to have been hardly mentioned
in subsequent meetings. Cabinet Secretary Sir Robert
Armstrong says: 'It wasn't discussed. Why should it be
discussed? The Prime Minister was very firm that it was
business as usual.'

'As I think you'd expect, it made people more determined to have normal government, not less,' says Charles
Moore, Mrs Thatcher's authorised biographer. 'And it
didn't make people revise their opinions. Nobody in the
Conservative government thought that you had to do
something very different now because of the bomb, either
in other respects or in relation to Ireland.'

Moore argues that there was 'a pause in the Anglo-Irish

process. But only a pause. It didn't deflect the drive for the Anglo-Irish Agreement, but there was a short period of doing nothing much and just… convalescing.'

The Troubles had been going on for sixteen years at this point. Cabinet Secretary Robert Armstrong was in the midst of diplomatic talks with his Irish counterpart Dermot Nally.

> [Armstrong's immediate reaction] was to wonder whether the whole process would be stopped. But then I realised, quite quickly realised, that she, Mrs Thatcher, would think that was a victory for the terrorists, if it stopped.
>
> It affected the negotiations, and she obviously felt that the process would have to slow down. She was very keen not to do anything which would seem as if she was conceding points which she mightn't otherwise have. She wrote on one bit of paper, 'this will all have to go rather slowly.' But she didn't want to stop it.
>
> They didn't slow down very much. So I think it was a politician's reaction in a situation of uncertainty, that you'd have to go a bit slower for a bit. I don't think there was anything more to it than that.

'I think it's an important point that it tended to reinforce her views of things rather than change… rather than turn them upside down,' says Margaret Thatcher's authorised biographer, Charles Moore.

> So in a way it strengthened her, though some might say it made [her views] more rigid, but it did strengthen her, because she always took the terrorist threat very, very seriously, and she always thought you had to fight it flat out. So this was proof in her mind that that's what you were dealing with. Whereas the sort of politician who's always thinking, 'Maybe the IRA aren't so bad after all', looking to put out feelers towards them, might feel differently. But she felt, 'I know they're evil bastards and now I'm… everyone can see they are.' I think that's more how she saw it. And that means that she's not sort of psychologically disturbed, because it's not undercutting her worldview.

'What are you doing tonight?' fireman Steve Tomlin's boss asked him one day. Tomlin wasn't doing anything of any significance.

'Right, go home, get your civilian clothes on – you're going out.'

'Where am I going?'

The senior officer didn't know – Tomlin just had to be at Roedean fire station, on the outskirts of Brighton, for a particular time.

'What do I tell my wife?'

'I don't know, because I don't know myself, but you're going out.'

When Tomlin arrived at Roedean fire station, he found that fellow Tebbit rescuer Fred Bishop was there, as was another colleague.

> And then, all we knew, we had to be at a certain service station or a point at a certain time, and then we had to phone a phone number, which we did. And then we were told to go somewhere else by a certain time. And then eventually it ended up, back door of Stoke Mandeville, and we were ushered in there, on the QT, with the thought of helping the recovery of the Tebbits.

'His physical state was very, very bad, but certainly his mental state was what [the doctors] were concerned with,' Bishop says.

> And that's why they asked us to go, because he'd

have to discuss the incident with us. The only thing we had in common, really. We got him talking. Afterwards, the doctors took us to one side and said, 'Ah, brilliant, he's opened up.' And a couple of days later they phoned us and said, 'Absolutely brilliant, it's done what we needed to get him coming back up again.'

Bishop also saw Margaret Tebbit at Stoke Mandeville. When he went into her room, she said excitedly: 'Fred, come here!' He went over to her bedside. She said: 'Look at this – watch.' She raised her arm, very slightly.

'Margaret, that's magic.'

'Yeah – but I can't put it down. Can you put it down for me?'

Bishop was impressed by Mrs Tebbit's sense of humour. He recalls her saying: 'I'm glad this happened to me, and not Norman, being severely damaged and becoming an invalid like this.'

'Margaret, that [attitude] is absolutely brilliant, that's wonderful,' Bishop said.

'No – he'd be impossible to live with.'

'There's a question about physical robustness, because one of the important things is that ministers work indescribably hard,' says Callum McCarthy. 'We mainly explained what was happening,' Andrew Lansley says. 'If there were issues that he wanted to be involved in, what was going on, and then just literally to communicate back to ministerial colleagues and officials what he thought about stuff.'

'Actually in some ways it was easier, because you had more time,' says Ruth Thompson.

> Even though the Secretary of State wasn't terribly well, so you weren't at him from nine in the morning till nine at night, you had more time to go and talk to him.
>
> He rationed his time, as I remember it. He said, 'I'm tired, I can't, I don't want to do any more now. I'll have a snooze and let's try again in a couple of hours.' Or, 'I don't want to think about that today', and 'Can it wait?'
>
> I don't remember him being confused or making decisions and you thought, 'That's not like him.' I remember it being pretty normal. I think more things were delegated, and he would just say, 'Oh, never mind, get Ken [Baker] to decide, or get Norman [Lamont] to decide, or get Paul [Channon] to decide.'* There were a few things like that, but a lot of things weren't

---

* Baker, Lamont and Channon were three of the DTI's junior ministers.

like that. I remember thinking, at various points, how odd it is that you can function in this way.

He seemed to me to be amazingly on the ball. It just shows the capacity of the human mind. I mean, I don't think it's confined to him, but he demonstrates this capacity, to compartmentalise things. He wanted to get on with those things. I may be projecting a bit, but it was almost [that] it made him feel normal. And most other things were not normal at all. So let's have the normal and make the most of it.

CHAPTER FOUR

'POSSIBLY THE BIGGEST CRIME, EVER'

'Probably straight away we worked on the basis of, let's operate as if it's a timer,' says Detective Inspector John Byford. 'The longest known timer that [the IRA had] used is three months.' Police decided to look at a time window of 104 days, from 1 July to 12 October.

The bomber might have been a registered hotel guest during this period. They might have simply visited a registered guest's room. Or they might have been a member of staff, a tradesman, or a delivery driver. Even if someone wasn't the bomber, they could have been an IRA person on reconnaissance. Or an innocent person who'd seen something which would turn out to be significant.

Detectives wanted to speak to everyone who'd been inside the hotel, for whatever reason, at any point during this 104-day window. But they didn't have in-hotel CCTV footage, or a complete set of credit card details. If anyone had given false details and paid in cash, they could be extremely hard to find. DCI Graham Hill says: 'At the outset, it seemed an enormous task, at the very outset.'

'I seem to remember at the time – and I'm going to say this – for the first time ever since I joined the police, I was perhaps a little bit bewildered,' says Detective Superintendent Bernie Wells.

> Because, as I say, nobody within Sussex [Police], certainly, had ever had to deal with an explosion. I was responsible, because I was the detective superintendent for that division. And therefore, any crime, my responsibility. And I'm very conscious that my knowledge was, to say limited, is putting it mildly. Was nil.
>
> Whereas normally I'd go to any scene, of any murder – and I've dealt with a lot in my time – full of confidence, knowing exactly what I'm going to do, picking up all the various points, and then picking

up the leads which we're going to follow. Here, it was totally, totally different. And I think it was for everybody. Because I remember, when I got back to the police station, another senior officer from the police station approached me. He said, 'Oh, have they examined the room? I just wondered if there were any fingerprints?' And I said, 'The room? There's no room there. It's gone.' In fairness to him, he hadn't visited the scene.

The 'Hotel Squad' put together a chart, with the list of rooms down one edge and the 104 days down the other. Using the hotel's handwritten registration cards, phone records, receipts, and other documents, they started work on their list of guests.

For each name they found, the first task was to find out 'are the people who they say they are, do they live where they say they live?' Detective Inspector John Byford says. 'And it could have been anywhere from Johannesburg to St Petersburg. And of course, lots of them were. So, was it a daunting task? Yes it was a daunting task. Was it doable? Yes it was, provided we had the staff to do it.'

Even before the bombing, Sussex Police had been stretched. Since that March, they'd been sending officers to miners' strike-affected counties. This had 'severely depleted the operational strength of the force,' the chief constable had noted shortly before the bombing.[27] There had also been 'five years of standstill budgets'.[28]

DI John Byford recalls that, during a murder investigation in April 1984, he decided he'd like some whiteboards in the incident room, and went down to see the admin person.

> Do you know, I couldn't even get bloody drawing pins and things out of these people, because there was no money. And eventually I got whiteboards put up on the wall in this office. And it was done with the attitude, 'Oh, well, that means we won't be able to spend money on so and so and so and so.' And yet, here we are, only six months later, when this bomb goes off… I won't say that money was no object – it just didn't come into it.

Detective Superintendent Bernie Wells agrees: 'Whatever we wanted, we got.'

For the crime-scene examiners, the day of the bombing had been 'one of, something we used to call "hurry up and wait", really,' Sussex officer Richard Lovett says. 'We had a lot of standing around and deliberating, as to, once we could get into the scene, how we were going to approach it.'

'We all sat there twiddling our thumbs,' says Met officer Bob Thorn.

> You're thinking, 'Well, what can we do?' What happens, not just with me but I've seen it with others, is that you actually, your brain locks up. It's so huge, you're not actually thinking straight; your brain is in overdrive. And [a colleague] actually gave me that little nudge, and said, 'Don't you think we should clear the pavements here, Bob?' Because there was debris lying around. I said, 'Yeah, thanks Ian, that's it.' So we cleared the pavements.

They also formed a line and started sweeping the beach. 'It was just in case any fragments of any evidence we'd wanted would have been on the beach front,' says DS Michael Colacicco.

> The other thing it did was show to people that actually there was a group of people that knew what we were doing. Because it drew attention. It was as daybreak [came], and you'd got a line of people in different types of clothes – because it was overalls,

> hardhats, boots – it looked like we'd got some sort
> of system. And we gradually began to take control
> [of the scene].

However, 'the fire brigade still wouldn't allow us access to the building' until the final missing guest had been accounted for, Colacicco recalls. She wasn't found until the evening of the following day – the Saturday.

'She'd been in a bathroom almost adjacent to where the bomb had gone off,' Colacicco says.

> I spoke to our bomb-disposal guy, and said: 'If you'd
> been in that bathroom and the bomb had gone off,
> where should we be looking for the body?' He did a
> few calculations and pointed us… We found the body
> in [a] wardrobe, after we'd pulled some rubble out.
>
> And the first reaction the fire brigade had was the
> fire commander shouting out, 'Right, six men with
> shovels; we'll get her out now.' We've got this stand-
> off, saying, 'You will not touch the body. We want
> a pathologist here, we want the body examined in
> situ, and we want to see what evidence we're going
> to get from that.'

In an unpublished memoir, Bob Thorn recalls this as having

been said more bluntly, by a detective constable: 'Oh, no, you don't, this is now a police murder scene so you can f*** off and take all of your men with you.'

While some forensics officers searched the main part of the hotel, others worked to clear the huge rubble pile in the basement. This involved shovelling debris into bins, and sending it to be thoroughly sifted at a specialist facility, where they would hopefully discover bomb components. Bob Thorn says: 'You've got to take the scene back to London. That's effectively what we're doing.'

As they worked, one officer 'actually was drawing diagrams of areas which had been cleared,' Richard Lovett recalls.

> Bearing in mind any forensic examination has got to be totally systematic and planned, we would have probably, at the end of the day, said, 'Right, we've cleared that area, that area, that area, tomorrow we will start on that area, that area and that area.' And that was how it went. And normally we would work to those areas each day, and we'd finish when that area had been cleared. And so certainly I was working twelve- or thirteen-hour days, getting back to Brighton [police station], having a shower there, because you were so filthy you daren't take it home

with you. And, get your overalls off, get showered, get home, something to eat. 'Hello, darling, hello, children, I'm going to bed now, I'll get up in the morning and say goodbye.' And that's it, and that was literally it, it was those sort of days. It was going home, eating, sleeping, getting up, back to work. I've never had such an intensive three weeks as I had then.

It was heavy, manual work, shifting hundreds of tons of debris. 'Bear in mind we're detectives, we're not builders,' Colacicco says. 'People were very tired. Because every night trying to get in a bath, when you can hardly move, and getting up the next morning and repeating it – physically it was gruelling.'

'It was tiring,' agrees Andy Griffiths, one of the Sussex officers who was called in to help the C13 forensics team, agrees. 'It was physical and tiring. But that's what you were there to do.'

The C13 officers were stationed at Lewes, about nine miles from the scene. One of the team, Tim Mitchell, recalls that 'we'd have our breakfast and then we'd go to the coach, and then we'd [be] met there by a traffic officer who had three envelopes. Each envelope contained a route, and we'd choose one envelope and we'd do that route into Brighton. And the reason behind that was we didn't want to be attacked by terrorists.'

His colleague Michael Colacicco says:

> You don't normally get, didn't in that time, the anti-terrorist branch going around as a group. Every single one of us had been involved in major investigations for some years; if you had taken out ten of us, you'd have probably stopped a dozen trials, because there'd be no evidence been able to be produced. So they used to escort us to and from the bomb scene, with an armed escort. We'd be kept at Lewes, at the police headquarters. That didn't stop us escaping, to go for meals in the evening.

Cracks were appearing in parts of the building, while they were working inside it, forensics detective Bob Thorn says. Health-and-safety people were on site, 'measuring how much it had moved overnight. By about the second day, we'd got a firm of builders to come in. And they watched our backs. They put [in] reinforcing rods, holding the floors up, in different places, to protect us. Because otherwise, the safety officers were saying, "You've got to get out."'

Michael Colacicco recalls an argument with a planning-department official, who tried to condemn the building and order the forensics team to leave. 'I threatened to arrest him for obstructing the police if he didn't piss off.'

Colacicco recalls a health-and-safety officer pointing to something in the basement:

> He said, 'That's blue asbestos and that's cracked, that's dangerous.' And went out to our control van and reported it. The local authority, or whatever, sent in people with spacesuits on, who then said, 'Yes, it is.' And they came back and issued us with some masks, which were crap. Up to that we'd used just filter, a piece of gauze with a steel plate over the front. These had things you screwed in at the side. But you couldn't work with them because, the amount of heavy work, they'd fill up with sweat on the inside and you'd drown.

The investigators 'invariably' had to take them off:

> You couldn't work with them. And we suffered quite badly with injuries, working in very hard conditions. So, I went into hospital there twice, with my hand being crushed and a split on the back of my head. But you're going back to an era when health and safety didn't exist, and no one ever complained of anything.

'I know we ate mince in various forms for a number of days,' says crime-scene investigator Tim Mitchell. Sussex officer Richard Lovett recalls that 'most of the time it was max packs and doggie bags. Max packs are those sort of instant-coffee things, you get them in various flavours – well, they have a different label on the front.'

At one point, the officers working on the scene were invited to a civic event being held nearby, DS Michael Colacicco recalls. They went along, 'decimated their buffet', and went back to work.

'I remember the briefing that when a bomb blows up, most of it still exists, and if you can find the important bits, it provides good evidence or intelligence as to who had made it,' says Sussex PC Andy Griffiths.

> It was a tremendously interesting thing to be involved in, absolutely. The morale was excellent. There were no grumbles. Police officers don't grumble when things are difficult and they're working hard. They tend to grumble more when things are boring. It was just such an important job, that people were absolutely focused on it. For me it was, it was exactly what I'd joined the police for. You were right there in the heart of one of the most serious investigations that [had] ever been conducted. I remember the

> importance of the mission was emphasised. And, of
> course, it wasn't all sweetness and light in terms of
> success, but I do remember that during the process
> we were told that things had been found, and so
> that was a morale boost.

'Obviously, there was a lot of shovelling,' Richard Lovett says. 'I don't remember getting bored about it. I think I always thought: "Keep scrabbling away, you're going to find something in a minute."'

The day after the bombing, *The Times* had called it 'the worst security blunder for many years'.[29] The *Daily Mirror* had used the phrase 'criminally complacent'.

'I remember once the chief constable had a press conference,' says Jon Buss, *The Argus*'s crime reporter.

> Walking through the aisle going down to the stage
> area, he stopped and looked at me and said, 'I very
> much enjoyed reading my obituary in *The Argus* this
> morning, Jon.' And of course I'd written, virtually
> a piece that said the chief constable is on the way
> out, because the police have made such a mess
> of the security. Which wasn't true, but it was sort of
> what was being written at the time.
>
> There was a press conference where he was asked

whether or not he was going to resign. That was on TV, as well, and his answer was on the lines that this isn't the time or place to discuss it. It wasn't a forceful response, it was a defensive response, and I think everybody could see that and sense the defensive way, and how it was getting to him. But that's not surprising. It would get to me, I think. And also because he had – and has – this great sense of duty. That's a good thing; he had this sense of duty, that he did feel personally responsible. And that must be a huge burden to bear.

'As the chief constable, the buck stops there,' Roger Birch says.

You know that, whatever has gone wrong in the organisation, it's your responsibility. And bear in mind I was a new boy, relatively. Not to being a chief constable, but a new boy in Sussex. Yeah, there were lonely times. In fact, I do remember, I think I'd not been to bed for thirty-six hours, and I went home, knackered, and my son phoned up, and said [jokingly], 'What the hell have you been up to now, Dad!' That boosted my morale.

Birch also recalls a phone call from his inspector of constabulary, saying, 'We heard you being pressed about resignation. Don't even think about it'. He says: 'So I had support from the inspector of the constabulary, and I also had support from the Home Secretary and members of Parliament. I was well supported.

> On the Saturday [13 October], Harold Macmillan and Julian Amery invited me to supper, and that was another exercise in backing up the local chief constable. We had a talk about the media, because, in the middle of the supper, I was called to the phone. It was my PRO [press officer], who said, 'We've got news that the Sunday papers are going to do a really scathing attack on you, for allowing all this lot to happen.' So, I went back in and Macmillan said, 'What was all that about, chief constable?' And I told him, and he said, 'Oh, well, what you've got to do is feed the papers for Monday.' We had a good chat about public relations and press relations. Again, it was a support effort.

In a profile piece headlined 'Police Chief in the Firing Line', Jon Buss was also sympathetic:

> Three weeks ago he was being hailed as the man who put the smile back into law enforcement. Today they are baying for his resignation. For Roger Birch, Chief Constable of Sussex, the events of Brighton's Bloody Friday have provided a reminder, if one were needed, that when you are at the top then the memories are short and the knives are long.

Birch, who had set up an independent inquiry soon after the bombing, once told Buss that 'I felt very lonely for a time but I never lost confidence in my team. I knew they would not be found wanting.' He was correct. The inquiry's report offered some criticisms, but did make it 'abundantly clear', Birch wrote, 'that nothing Sussex Police might reasonably have been expected to do against the situation prevailing at the time, would have prevented the explosion.'[30]

Sussex officer Roger Mead says:

> It's almost complete lockdown now, isn't it, when they have a conference. Up until then, you had to balance the freedom for people who wanted to protest outside with the freedoms of MPs that wanted to come and go to their conference, but maintain policing, and policing's a very fine

balance. It's when it goes wrong that then, of course, everybody wants to pick it apart, and you get these nine o'clock juries the next morning saying, 'Why didn't they do this, why didn't they do that?' Well, the reason they didn't do it was because it had never been done before and it never happened before. You can't have a magic ball.

'More than 120 detectives are now working on the bombing, which was today branded by police as possibly the biggest crime ever,' Jon Buss wrote on 19 October. Another *Argus* article from the week after the bombing claimed that Brighton police station 'will never [be] busier. No one ambles along its hive of corridors these days. Everything is urgent. Messages flash from room to room. Phones ring continuously.'

'I think there were three things' contributing to the sense of urgency, Sussex detective Dave Gaylor says.

The fact it was the government. There was the watch of the world – the whole world was watching what was going on, so you were under that type of scrutiny. You had the scrutiny of the media and the television companies and the commentators. And then, of course, the most important, the fact there

was a live IRA cell operating in the UK that needed
to be traced, before they killed again. So that was
the core driver.

'Although I didn't personally believe that they tried to
kill Margaret Thatcher,' Detective Superintendent Bernie
Wells says,

that's got to be the opinion that I take on board.
When I'm dealing, or when anyone's dealing, with
any murder, I guess, you're feeling the pressure for
the family. And this case, we're feeling the pressure
for the country. I mean, they've tried to murder our
Prime Minister, for goodness' sake.

Before anyone could be eliminated from suspicion, DCI
Graham Hill says,

We needed to have their full identity. We needed
to be satisfied who they were, we needed to look
into where they lived. We would run them on a
search, which would mean we'd be looking for any
convictions they'd got, we'd be looking for any intelligence about them. We'd probably have wanted
to cross-reference that against a database of any

known terrorists or people with sympathies, the kind of political stuff that you always would do. So, trying to see whether this person had any links to terrorist organisations.

We would want to establish exactly when they stayed there, we would want to know who they were staying there with, we would want to know what their patterns were, did they use the restaurant, do they remember anyone else who was there, did anything unusual happen when they were there. I mean, pretty standard stuff around leading us up to being able to say, 'Well, we're as sure as we can be that there's absolutely no reason why Mr Jones from 14 the High Street, who's come away with his wife for three days in Brighton, there's absolutely nothing to suggest that there's anything more to it than that.'

'They weren't short interviews,' says DC Mike Stone, who went around the home counties taking statements from hotel guests.

You would go through, chronologically, what they did since they walked into the Grand Hotel. There was no average time to interview someone. It had to be done, and if it took two hours, or it took eight hours, that's what it took.

It was, 'Who were you with, what did you do, did any ... did you have anybody in your room, did any staff come into your room, can you describe the member of staff?' You try to be as thorough as you can, and just go through their stay totally, and paint a picture.

Joe Public never has that great a memory. But they all wanted to [help], yeah. A lot of people were affronted by the fact someone had tried to blow up the government, basically. And there were a lot of people, certainly a lot of people that we interviewed – because we are talking the Grand Hotel, of course, you are talking a certain section of society. They wanted this guy caught. They were only too happy to... I mean, we interviewed one guy and stayed for lunch. It was on a Sunday. 'Sit down, officers, have some Sunday lunch with me and my family. Let's have a break, we'll have some lunch, and then we'll carry on after lunch.' Wonderful.

Though he tried to create a relaxed atmosphere during these interviews, Stone, [would never say] 'You're not a suspect.' Because everybody was a suspect. Can't say that. Just say, 'We're from the incident team, Brighton police station, investigating the Brighton bomb. We understand you stayed at the hotel during this period, we'd like to talk to you about it, if that's OK?' That's the sort of thing you would start it with. And some people would say, 'Am I a suspect?' I would say, 'We would like to eliminate you from our inquiry.' Because really, that's what an inquiry is, of such a scale; it's a process of elimination.

Part of the John Street building was designated the 'major-incident room'. 'It was part, in those days, electronic and part paper,' DCI Graham Hill recalls.

It was the hub of information coming in and going out, and everything had to go through, apart from some of the sensitive intelligence which would have been given to us on paper. But everything else had to come through the major-incident room. And within that room you have inputters, you have telephone operators for taking telephone calls, you have researchers, you have statement readers. So you've got a hub of people that are collecting the information in, that are recording the information that's coming in.

And how the statement reading works is, let's just take as an example, I interview you, let's say, and you give me a story about something. The statement reader goes through and marks on the statement everything which needs to be verified. Which is everything.

So you say to me, 'I was working in Boots the chemist at four o'clock this afternoon', the action will be, check the person was working at the chemist at that time. Goes on a bit further and they say, 'I then got in my car and drove home.' And there'll be an action, check car number, were there any speeding fines, any parking tickets issued for that car number at that time. And then so on and so forth. So there'd be a statement reader that's specifically doing that. That statement reader would be overseen by, normally a detective inspector, [who] runs that room. That person would be the eyes and ears of anything of significance that was coming in. Anything of significance at all would get referred through to the senior investigating team.

'It must have been a week, ten days into the investigation,

and I'd gone downstairs in the Grand Hotel for something,' says crime-scene investigator Richard Lovett. 'There wasn't anybody about, and there shouldn't have been. I found this guy just wandering about, looking a bit lost downstairs.'

'Who are you?'

'Oh, I'm from the *Sunday Express*.'

'What are you doing in here?' Lovett asked, wondering how he got past the PC guarding the perimeter.

'Oh, your chief superintendent told me...'

'I don't think he did, I think we'd have known about it. What's his name?'

'Oh, you know him, the guy.'

'No, what's the name of my chief superintendent?'

The journalist had no answer.

> I marched him out and took him to the PC on the gate, and apparently he'd spun some line to him, hadn't even asked for credentials. I think that was a one-off isolated case. Obviously you have to report it. And, so I told this guy, I said, 'Well, look, the first thing we'll want is every stitch of clothing you've got on you.'
>
> He went a bit white at that. I said, 'Well, I'm sorry, but you've entered the scene of a major

> crime, an unauthorised entry, we don't know now
> what evidence...' Pretty damn sure by then most of
> the evidence, any decent evidence had... we'd found
> and it had been taken away. But, the lengths that
> you guys go to to get a story at times.

In the U-bend of a toilet, in room 329 of the Grand Hotel, on 27 October, a C13 detective constable found something. The toilet was muddy – a combination of debris, dust and water – but he 'spread the mud out on the floor', revealing the object. Though it had been bent 'into the shape of an ice-cream cone', he knew straight away what it was.[31] It was a piece of Memo Park Timer. These were one-hour timers used by motorists to remind them when their parking was about to run out. They were also known to have been used by bomb makers as safety mechanisms.

The exhibits that the forensics examiners logged as evidence included: 'Yellow sponge with green scourer', 'Brighton area telephone directory' and 'box of matches'.[32] They took anything of any conceivable relevance.

'You always do at any crime scene, you take away absolute rubbish at times,' Sussex officer Richard Lovett says.

> It's like, you empty the kitchen bin, 'contents of
> kitchen bin'. Because, if you don't get it then, and

it turns out it's something significant a month or so down the line, you've lost it. So you get it, and you take it back to your exhibit store. Sometimes someone will come along and say, 'Oh, we've had a word with one of the witnesses and they said they saw the offender putting something in the kitchen bin.' I mean, hopefully, if it's a murder weapon or something you'd have found it in the contents of the kitchen bin when you empty it, but, it could be what appeared on a relevant piece of paper, or something like that, at the time. So yes, you would have had your box of matches and your scourer and that sort of thing, whether they were relevant or not.

Having made 'several significant finds'[33] over the course of the two-and-a-half-week investigation, the crime-scene investigators packed up on 30 October. They had collected 880 tons of debris.

'Huge areas that had been absolutely piled high with debris were cleared,' Sussex officer Paul Solis recalls. 'In the kitchens, down in the basement, for instance, when you first looked down there, it was just rubble. And then at the end of the three weeks, it was, I wouldn't say spotless, but, there was floor space and everything. A huge amount of work had been done.'

They celebrated by forming a line and walking into the sea together. 'It's in the newspapers, a picture of the guys who did the scene wading into the sea on the last day,' DS Michael Colacicco says. 'What it's not telling you in the picture is, the boots filling up with water and some of the guys nearly drowning and having to be pulled out. Welly boots, they're steel capped, they don't come off that easily. You go into the sea and they fill up. And it was [a] rough sea, they were being pulled out.'

There was a young man who'd worked in the Grand's kitchens for a couple of weeks under a false name. There was a 'short, stocky man' seen running from the scene after the explosion. There was a man with a bag who, a witness claimed, 'was very peculiar and said he hated the Tories'. There were two conference security passes that had been found to have gone missing. There were the Irish people who'd been spotted, before the explosion, 'jeering at the Tories' at another hotel. Leads like this were not rare. Within a week of the bombing, police had received 'over 1,400 messages' from the public.[34]

'Was this the IRA's bomber?' read the front-page headline in *The Argus*, on 19 October. The police had released an artist's impression of a man with a long beard and a case under his arm. 'A young chambermaid' had seen the 'bearded mystery man' letting himself into room 629 a few days before the bombing. He was not the IRA's bomber.

'There'll always be people that... it's a bit like Alfred Hitchcock, when he used to appear in his films, he'd just be a fleeting glimpse, as a doorman or getting onto a train,' says Detective Constable Dave Gaylor. 'You always have these people that will walk across the crime scene somewhere, and either they're hard to track down, or when you actually find them they've got no relevance to what you're investigating, but for a time they can be quite important. And for an investigation this big, there'll always be those scenarios.'

'False leads about people who had stayed in the hotel, false leads about things that might have seemed relevant...' Graham Hill says.

> I'm sure I wouldn't exaggerate by saying there were thousands of those. I can't specifically remember any, because it's such a frequent occurrence on these types of major inquiries that you get many false leads, and what you do is try to resolve them. Obviously you speak to that person, you find out what their explanation is, you quickly rule them out in most cases. And then you can close that lead off and move onto the next one.

Any lead like that, you take seriously, and try and resolve it. You always do in these inquiries, and there's a good reason for that. Where the police come into possession of information which would have an impact on the inquiry, then they're under a legal obligation to disclose it to the defence.

So, let's just say, for example, somebody had come forward and said, 'I saw somebody walking into the hotel around the period in time, carrying a suspicious-looking bag, and – let's just say – speaking in an Irish accent.' Then we would be duty-bound to follow it up. We'd want to follow it up anyway. If we didn't follow it up then the defence at any trial are going to say, 'Well, what about this inquiry, why didn't you do anything about it?' So you have a huge operation that, in 99 per cent of the cases, is going to take you absolutely nowhere. You do have to follow those leads up.

'Obviously, we were working very closely with forensic teams, and particularly specialists in the area of bombs, and how bombs are put together, with time and power units and delay devices,' says Graham Hill.

Initially, we weren't sure – I mean in the first couple

of days, we weren't sure – it could have been any sort of bomb, it could have been literally left there five minutes before, it could have been triggered by some sort of electronic device at the time. But, obviously, working closely with the forensic teams and the explosive teams, it soon, it very soon became apparent that the device that had been left had a delay capability. So that, we knew pretty soon that we weren't looking at the actual day the bomb went off, we were probably having to go back some length of time.

One of [the IRA's] favoured devices, probably their favoured device at the time, was using a time and power unit, a TPU, which has a – it was explained to me in great detail because I, prior to this, knew nothing about TPUs – but has a capability of delaying the detonation of your explosive by a very fixed period of time.

'Fairly quickly, we discovered that an arms cache had been found in a forest in Northamptonshire,' says Detective Superintendent Bernie Wells. It contained some devices – timers, apparently – which 'were numbered one to seven, and number four... there was no number four. So we, because of all the other information which we got, we quickly thought to ourselves, that could have been the one used.'

'Probably within the first two weeks, we were pretty sure that it was a 24-day power device,' Graham Hill says.

> You couldn't rule out that there was a reconnaissance before, you couldn't rule out that somebody had even gone in there afterwards. But the priority of the search to track down people was obviously for that time, when we knew the bomb was put down.
>
> And also we were pretty sure by then, I'd say almost certain, it was [placed in] room 629. So those two very important facts, obviously, were the hub of the inquiry.

Detective Constable Mike Stone was sent to interview lots of people who were obviously not the Brighton bomber. 'I won't call it dull,' he says.

> It's mundane. But it's necessary. We were well aware that some of it was going to be repetitive, boring. And my own personal view is, but I knew it had to be done. I think the biggest, the most important thing, and the thing that kept me going a lot was, you could quickly tell that this guy's not the one, in

your own mind, but until you actually interviewed him you didn't know what information he had, which he didn't know might be of relevance.

'You never knew. Somebody who might have been staying on the same floor could have just walked past at a core time and seen something,' Sussex officer Dave Gaylor says.

There could have been a member of staff who saw something; there could have been a delivery person. So you had to try and cover everything, although a lot of the investigation wasn't needed at the end of the day. But it had to be thorough, just in case, because you never know what questions you're going to get asked later on, and it then could be two, three, four years later, and it could be too late to go back.

'There would have been considerable inquiries put into every member of staff that was working there at the time, and had been working there before, and was working there at the time the bomb actually went off,' DCI Graham Hill says.

We'd have had a full list of all staff, they will all have been interviewed, we'll have done background checks on them, we'd have listened for any tittle tattle, we'd have encouraged anybody that knew anything to come forward. If they were suspicious of another member of staff, we were trying to create the environment that they felt they could come forward.

John Byford addressed the hotel staff early in the investigation.

They weren't happy. Lost their jobs, hadn't they? I mean, they weren't happy people at all. And I think some of them even lived in the hotel as well. And, if they were going to get work, it wasn't going to be necessarily in Brighton. I was virtually saying to them, 'You ain't going to leave Brighton till we've done this, so please, don't think about that.'

But I felt quite happy, after my chat to them, that they accepted, having been told the story, they felt then included in what we're doing. One or two of them were Irish, actually, and they spoke to me afterwards. With the assistance of some of the hotel staff we put together a list of names and addresses [which we] used as a priority, so that we, perhaps within the space of a week or ten days, had probably interviewed all of them.

'We used to get the hotel staff into the police station, update them on what the latest was and say, "Anybody know anything about this or that?"' Bernie Wells says.

> And, yeah, some of them did come forward with bits and pieces – nothing that took us anywhere, but we regularly had meetings. We would update them, where we were, and then say, 'Right, now can anybody remember who was in that room?' Those sorts of questions. And gradually, little bits and pieces filtered through, and then we would put it to them again. They were excellent. They wanted to help, they wanted to do all they could to bring the person to book.

Sussex DC Paul Gibbon recalls interviewing an elderly housekeeper at the Grand:

> [she had] worked in the hotel for years and years. She was interesting, because her life was the Grand Hotel, and she lived in the staff quarters there. But she was responsible for [room] 629. I can remember interviewing her, and she [said] one day she went in there, obviously during the occupancy of Roy Walsh, and she noticed that the bath panel had been moved,

because there were grease marks around it. So that was kind of one of the first corroborative times that we got information, or we were able to corroborate that yes, this is where the bomb had been placed.

Another interesting thing was, whether it was her or one of the waiters, that they recall[ed] delivering a bottle of vodka to the room. And the significance of the vodka is not that he drank it, but he [may have] used it to wash his hands. Because that was standard IRA practice at the time, that when they'd handled explosives they would use spirit to wash their hands, to get rid of the nitroglycerin, or the explosive traces [from] their fingers.

Police officers who weren't working on the investigation, like PC Simon Parr, were told 'absolutely not a syllable' about how it was going, he recalls.

And you wouldn't expect to. The Russians have a saying that if two people know something, it isn't a secret. And if you are dealing with something of that nature, something of that sensitivity, the audacity, the planning, the careful thought that's gone into it, the last thing you want is to give any hint or suggestion you might have a name.

The investigation, and everything to do with it, was so far away from those of us who were on the ground and charged with normal day-to-day policing that it could almost have happened in Paris or Bangkok or Amsterdam. It was just so far away from us. Just there were parts of the building we couldn't use.

John Byford recalls that, shortly before Christmas, he and a colleague were sent to Belfast to get some intelligence from the Royal Ulster Constabulary, about two potential suspects. An RUC man told them, 'I have the information that you've come for, but I am instructed that I've got to give it to you in this sealed brown envelope. And this sealed brown envelope is addressed to Jack Reece.'

Byford says now: 'So, we've been all the way over to Ireland, and we come away with a brown envelope. It gives you an idea of the concern about information getting into the wrong hands at the wrong time.'

Hotel guests from outside the UK were traced through Interpol. John Byford ended up sending 1,300 requests through DCI Roger Mead, deputy bureau chief at Interpol London. These inquiries came back with a 'less than 1 per cent failure rate, which is quite unique,' Mead says.

Inquiries in countries that weren't part of Interpol – like South Africa, Dubai, and East Germany – were done 'on a personal basis,' through contacts Mead had built up.

> You see, policing is policing all over the world, it's not a very different job wherever you go. Policemen have got the same problems, be it dealing with motorists or terrorists or whatever. And there's a sort of, like a brotherhood of policing, and there's ways to get things done. There was sometimes a little bit of politics where people challenged the inquiry, as to whether it was political. In some countries they weren't quite sure whether [the IRA] were terrorists or whether they were a republican army. And under the Interpol charter, of course, you don't deal with political things. I recall a couple of queries about 'is this political?' And no, it had been judged it certainly wasn't political, it was a murder inquiry. And it was a criminal inquiry.
>
> But, no, we didn't get much response from Interpol Dublin. They considered [that] to try and destroy the British government was a political act by the IRA, and they chose not to deal with those inquiries. But the security services would be working closely with the people at Brighton. Things in Ireland

weren't a difficulty for them, they had their ways
of dealing with that.*

Various people had stayed at the Grand Hotel 'allegedly
with their wives or husbands or whatever, where they
were not,' DI John Byford says. 'That was amusing, it was
interesting, and also it held up the work, because you had
to very often do a double inquiry, because they weren't
prepared to tell you the truth.'

Several people turned out to have written false names
on their registration cards, for this kind of reason. Some
of these had given other details which were correct – like
their real address, or perhaps a car number plate; some
had phoned home from their rooms. Others had to be
traced by appeals through the press.

Chief Constable Roger Birch says:

> I remember [an Assistant Chief Constable] telling
> me, 'Well, we're getting a bit of resistance, about
> people saying who they've been with, or whatever,
> because we've found various articles of ladies'
> underwear in places we shouldn't have expected to

---

* Mead doesn't recall receiving that many inquiries relating to the
Republic of Ireland anyway.

find them.' And [he] made a broadcast, really saying, 'Look, some of you may have found yourself, people we'd like to talk to, in an embarrassing situation because of people you've been with, or guests you've had in your room. But we promise you, if you come forward, it will be kept totally confidential.' That had to be done.

'There were floods of people coming to the police station when they were going through the hotel cards,' PC Chris Cox recalls. 'Lots of "Mr Smiths" coming in to be interviewed.'

'Not everybody wanted to be interviewed at home,' DC Mike Stone says. 'We had some interesting locations to meet people, shall we say, and leave it at that.'

'One of the problems with this sort of inquiry,' DCI Graham Hill says:

We had this problem from the outset – is you get all sorts of people that remember all sorts of things. The police always rely on people coming forward, and that's really very often how murders and other crimes get cleared. But within the middle of that you have to deal with an awful lot of what I would call red herrings. And you might have, for example, a porter in the hotel that remembered seeing a chap acting a bit strange by the lift or seeming agitated in the restaurant, or whatever it might be.

You have to be very careful about how you deal with that sort of information. You have to deal with definites and positives, things that you're absolutely sure about. You have to be very careful about over-egging things that turn out to be wrong, because it will set the whole thing off on an entire different area. And of course – have you been a pressman before?

OK, well, you can take it from me, pressmen will jump on anything in this sort of inquiry, so if you produce a photo-fit of someone who was acting strangely by the lift, they will jump in and say, 'This is the Brighton bomber.' The problem of course is it may well not be the Brighton bomber, and that's the juggle that, when you're a senior investigating officer on these sorts of inquiries, you have to balance up the benefit against where it's going to send you off on a complete tangent. You can't really be right, because if it turned out to be the Brighton bomber then someone will obviously say, 'Well, why didn't you publish?'

David Tadd ran a team of fingerprint experts at Scotland

Yard, who exclusively handled terrorist cases. They had a range of physical and chemical processes that they would use to reveal fingerprints which weren't visible to the naked eye; these would be done in sequence. First the material would be exposed to a series of light sources – laser, UV and infra-red. Then there were two chemical processes. The ninhydrin test reacts to certain types of amino acids in sweat; 'physical developer' reacts to certain kinds of proteins.

Once the registration cards came in, Tadd's team would put them through this process, eliminate any prints left by hotel staff, and then see what was left. They had a set of fingerprints on file, of known and suspected terrorists. The team would sit round a table, and look at a particular registration card, comparing the marks on the card with their file prints. There was no computer pattern-recognition technology. This was all done by visual inspection: putting them side by side and staring at them, looking for 'patterns within the patterns'. It was a time-consuming process, even once they started solely focusing on cards from room 629.[35]

An IRA convict, who was in prison, was believed to have made, or received, a suspicious number of phone calls around the time of the bombing, Detective Constable Paul Gibbon recalls.

And the suggestion was that obviously he had prior knowledge of what was going to go on. So Graham Hill and I travelled down to [the prison]. And the significance of it for me is that [the IRA man] was suspected of the Harrods bombings.

And one of the police officers killed at Harrods was a friend of mine. We used to play football together, we used to go for drinks together. So there I am, you can imagine the emotions of travelling down to see somebody who I know potentially killed a friend of mine. And being able to do absolutely nothing about it.

So, we go down there, and he refuses to come out of his cell. And, so, as it was in those days, it was before human-rights acts and everything, the security personnel went and dragged him out of his cell, and brought him in and sat him down in front of us. We're sitting one side of the table, this *person* is sitting the other. And he's doing classic anti-interrogation, and he looks at the wall and says, 'I'm not talking to the likes of yous.' And that was it.

That's all he said: 'I'm not talking to the likes of yous.' And so my emotions, I want to get up and f**king kill the guy. Emotionally for me, I will say, that's something that's lived with me, well, for the rest of my life.

On Sunday 4 November, preparations were underway for the CBI's annual conference, at Eastbourne's Grand Hotel, which Mrs Thatcher was due to attend. Sussex police dog-handler Les Jeavons was called in to search the hotel.

I went up – I think it was probably about the first floor. I went into a bathroom, and I lifted the lid off the toilet cistern, and inside there I found a tin, Quality Street tin, with black tape all round it, and some wires.

Right. I left the lid off, get a bit of tape, tie it and I walk out, letting the tape go and out through the entrance. So that when the bomb-disposal people come, you don't say, 'Oh, you go up these stairs you turn left and it's the third door on the right and you go in the room and it's the second door over here.' They just follow the tape, right.

And, anyway, once I'd found it, everybody was cleared out of the hotel, bomb-disposal units were called down, they then wanted a 200-yard exclusion zone put round it, which meant other hotels, and people all round this big hotel in Eastbourne had to be evacuated. They went in, disrupted it and it was just a hoax, I think to see if we were still doing our job properly.' *The Times* reported that Sussex Police 'closed the surrounding area for most of the day. The tin was found to be stuffed with paper.'[36]

The chart on the Hotel Squad's wall was useful in terms of morale. Detective Inspector John Byford recalls that:

> on a daily basis, you could see, all the time, that you were making progress. That sounds pretty basic, but there's a big element of truth in it. I can remember one particular member of the staff, she'd tell you that she'd filled in twenty-four boxes that day, or something like that, which would be tremendous. And, for her, a great sense of achievement, that's what we've done today, we've cleared twenty-four out of the three thousand.

However, this was negative information – so-and-so wasn't involved. For three months, investigators had little or no positive information about who was involved. Even when they were fairly sure they knew when the guest had stayed, and in which room. The relevant registration card contained a false name and address.

The mood, though, remained optimistic, DCI Graham Hill says.

> I've run many inquiries, and I can say that with almost every inquiry that I've been involved in, even after long periods of time, there's still that motivation. There's always something happening, and you might feel one day, I don't know if this is going anywhere, and the next day something happens and you're all on that enthusiastic roll again.
>
> When you've done three or four weeks of working monster hours… exciting's not the right word, but I always think, looking back on those sorts of inquiries, there's always that optimistic determination that you're going to catch the person that's done it.
>
> You get highs and lows, of course. You get times when things don't seem to be going in the direction you want them to go. But then something happens, and you go off in another direction and it generates a momentum. So I think it's a sort of momentum, but I don't know, excitement – I guess there is excitement in there somewhere, but it's probably not the word I would use.

His colleague Paul Gibbon, though, does call it 'exciting'.

'You're working on almost every detective's dream, in some ways,' says Gibbon.

> Somebody has committed what is essentially a treasonable offence. My recollection is that there was certainly some underlying resentment, quite rightly so, I think, from the detectives, certainly at Brighton, who were left having to run the CID office, doing, like, the mundane burglaries and assaults, to us lucky buggers that were on the inquiry team.

'I felt under pressure, no two ways about that,' says Detective Superintendent Bernie Wells.

> You've always got to be optimistic, particularly when you're in charge, because you've got to convey to the others that you're full of enthusiasm and optimistic. Whether I was optimistic... I would guess I was, I'm that sort of person. But it was perhaps sometimes difficult. Because we weren't sort of, really making progress. There was bits and pieces, names thrown up. But no, we never really, until we identified [the suspect], we never really had anything.
>
> Normally, there's little things keep cropping up, and each morning, you say, 'Right, I can tell you

today, yesterday we discovered that...' That didn't apply in this case. It was difficult. Difficult to find something to engender more enthusiasm, because that's obviously what you're trying to do. But I don't think it was needed. I think everyone was just dedicated to finding out who did it.

CHAPTER FIVE

THIS GUY'S OF EXTREME INTEREST

By early November, Sussex Police's Hotel Squad were paying particular attention to one of the guest-registration cards. The guest had given false details:

Name: Walsh, Roy

Address: 27 Braxfield Road, London, SE4

Nationality: English

'I personally went up there and visited that address,' Detective Superintendent Bernie Wells says. 'And the people there had been there a few years. And we traced the people before them, and no one had ever heard of Roy Walsh, who'd lived at that address.'

'That focused our interest,' DCI Graham Hill says. 'Particularly when the evidence around the location of the bomb came up, and the timing of the bomb, because we knew he was in that room at the time. And lo and behold, it's a false address, and almost certainly a false name. So it's not particularly rocket science to say, this guy's of extreme interest.'

'Extensive inquiries have been made to trace this man,' John Byford wrote later.

> House to house inquiries were made in the Braxfield Road area and at business premises and social establishments in the vicinity. When these also proved negative, extensive use was made of the media publishing the name, address and handwriting of the man WALSH and requesting this person to come forward. A poster setting out this information was circulated to every police station in the UK.

Patrol, the Sussex Police newspaper, later noted:

> Working on the assumption that he would not have checked in without some form of identification, they checked the passport office, DVLC, births, deaths and marriages for reissues in the name of Roy Walsh.

> In the case of birth certificates, they had to look at
> 750,000 reissues which were stored in date order
> rather than alphabetical. There were many people
> called Roy Walsh who came to light in the course
> of the inquiry and all of these had to be followed
> up and eliminated.[37]

Interviews with potential witnesses provided 'practically no information' about Roy Walsh, DCI Graham Hill says. 'In fact I don't think there was any information at all, about somebody remembering either the person particularly booking in or indeed what he looked like.'

'We found the person who booked him in, but they couldn't remember him, of course,' Bernie Wells says.

> [The mystery guest] had vodka delivered to the
> room, and we found the waiter who actually took
> the vodka up to the room, and again, he couldn't
> really remember anything. And then, we know
> that two people from that room had a meal in the
> restaurant. Now, we plotted up that restaurant, and
> we found everybody in that restaurant, except those
> two people at the table.
>
> And I'll always remember this, everyone seemed
> to remember everybody except those two. 'Oh, yes,

on the next table was a man, woman and a young child.' 'What about that…', 'I can't remember who was on that table, I can't remember anybody.' But we know they were there because they had a meal, and put it on their bill.

Detective Constable Andy Young recalls being sent to the taxi rank at Brighton railway station to canvass drivers. One of them remembered taking someone who might have been Walsh from the station to the Grand Hotel. 'I don't know if it was actually useful, but it fills a little bit of the story in,' Young says. 'Without doing it, you don't know what you're going to obtain, do you?'

Once Roy Walsh had been found to have given a false address, David Tadd's fingerprint team had focused almost exclusively on his registration card. It had been subjected to the usual light sources, to try to reveal faint marks, but nothing was visible. The first of two chemical tests had also proved fruitless. The second, however, had uncovered two fragmentary prints: the side of a palm, and the tip of a finger.

With the team checking these against file prints, by visual inspection, a suspected match was eventually found. The officer passed it up to their superior to check. The senior officer agreed, and passed it up to Tadd. Tadd confirmed the identification, and wrote, by hand, a report detailing this. It was so confidential that, when he took it to the typing pool, he left off the suspect's name. He added it later in biro.

On 18 January, Sussex CID chief Jack Reece and his colleague Bernie Wells went to Scotland Yard for a meeting. They'd been told beforehand that it concerned an important development, but weren't told what it was. Up to this point, bits and pieces of information had been coming through, but Sussex really had no idea who Roy Walsh was. David Tadd stood up and announced his discovery: the fingerprint of known IRA operative Patrick Magee, on the Roy Walsh registration card.

'It was about this time that Metropolitan Police had obtained a warrant for the arrest of Evelyn Glenholmes,' Bernie Wells says, dictating from notes of a talk he used to give in police circles.

> Unfortunately, the newspapers made certain disclosures about the warrant having been obtained for the arrest of this woman, and as a result of that publicity and further publicity generated from it, Glenholmes disappeared. Therefore, obviously, under no circumstances could we allow a leak to the press, that we had now identified Walsh. We realised that

this was going to be difficult because of all the publicity and help that we'd received from the media. It was decided at that time that the information we'd got would not go outside those persons present at the meeting.

A further meeting, on 21 January, according to Wells's notes, eventually concluded that the whole team working on the investigation should actually be told about Magee. Wells says:

> Some people were saying, 'Oh, you can't do that; you tell the team, it'll be bloody leaked, and he'll go to ground and we'll never find him, like Evelyn Glenholmes. There was a lot of soul searching over whether to release it. And we did release it to the whole team, I remember.
>
> We thought, well, they've all been working long hours, and hard, everybody on the team, and to keep it from them. Because there hadn't been any light at the end of the tunnel. Normally when you've got an investigation, there's a lead, and there's a lead, and there's a lead. There hadn't been anything. And you've got a job to keep people's, to keep officers' enthusiasm going, because they're thinking, 'Oh,

this isn't going anywhere.' So we thought, we've got to tell them, because they've all worked so hard for so long.

Fellow detectives Graham Hill and Paul Gibbon both recall this differently – that only a select few of the team were told. Hill says: 'I think the team were aware of the fact that there'd been an identification made, but that the actual detail of that identification, for a time anyway, was withheld from the team.' It was certainly withheld from journalists and the public. Police officers who weren't working on the inquiry, even senior ones, weren't told.

'You wanted to tell everybody,' Wells says. 'I remember even at Brighton police station, when other senior officers would say, "No news, Bernie – nothing?" [I'd say] "No." And I'm thinking, "You liar…"'

Chief Constable Roger Birch had to swallow a certain amount of pressure from those who weren't in on the secret – for example, the board of the Sussex Police Authority. How is the case going? Are you anywhere near solving it? Birch recalls: 'You say, "Well, yes, we are making extremely good progress." You just keep waffling away like that, don't you?'

'In the past year members of the four-to-five person [IRA] unit have visited the Grand Hotel frequently, have stayed as guests, have mingled with delegates to many other conferences, familiarised themselves with every detail of the hotel's lay-out,'[38] the Irish *Sunday Press* had claimed, two days after the bombing. Whether or not this was true, the possibility of reconnaissance was one reason why the investigation had to carry on, even after they'd identified Magee.

And the work had to be seen to be carrying on, DC Paul Gibbon says. 'Because, if the police had have stopped it, then the press would have got wind of it. And then start asking questions – well, why are they not doing those inquiries that they were doing before? Have they traced everybody?'

Publicly, Sussex CID chief Jack Reece kept up the charade that he didn't know who Roy Walsh was. On 27 January, more than a week after Magee's fingerprint had been identified, *The Observer* reported that 'peculiarities' in Roy Walsh's handwriting might give a clue as to his identity. Reece was quoted as saying: 'The way in which he completed the letter "E" on his hotel registration card has led to suggestions that he could be left handed.' *The Times* reported that in April, at the inquest into the deaths, 'Mr Reece said the description of Walsh was too imprecise to be released.'[39]

'I don't know of a reporter who's better in terms of

his contacts,' *Argus* news editor Chris Oswick says of his crime reporter Jon Buss.

> Jon's contacts with the police were such that if there was an overnight murder, say, a body found, anywhere in the Brighton area or most of Sussex, overnight, Jon would come in at half past seven, Jon would not only be able to put together a story, but would have a clear steer on the kind of murder that we were looking at, whether it was a stranger murder, a domestic murder, a drugs-related murder, or whatever.

Buss says:

> In those days, people like me had personal relationships with these detectives. We'd play snooker with them, we'd go to pubs with them, we'd get drunk with them. We would talk to them when they were divorcing their wives. I was part of the group, part of the set. They would ring me up, tell me about murders, at six, seven o'clock in the morning. Because they knew that if they get a good show in the first edition of *The Argus*, good witness appeals would get... this is before social media – the only

way that you would get a police appeal in the paper
is by knowing someone like me, and making sure
that I had information that would be helpful.

So I had a good personal relationship with dozens
of detectives. They knew what was going on in my
life, and I knew what was going on in their lives. Yes,
I was going to find out stuff that other people didn't
find out, but with [this investigation], it was the
bits and pieces around it, the Brighton connections.
I didn't know that this huge operation was going
on to track and arrest an IRA terror cell, which is
what was happening.

The *Daily Mail* got a tip off, apparently 'from a Dutch
journalist', about a possible IRA terrorist called Magee.
'The *Mail* dispatched a top news reporter and a photographer to try and talk to "Mr Magee", the paper's crime
reporter, Peter Burden, later wrote. 'They were met with a
barrage of rubbish thrown at them from above.'[40]

Somehow, Burden figured out that Magee was the
prime suspect for the Brighton bombing. Chief Constable
Roger Birch recalls:

He phoned Jack Reece, and said words to the effect,
'We understand you're looking for somebody called

Patrick Magee.' And Reece had the sense not to deny it, but said, 'If you break this now, you'll destroy one of the most important criminal investigations that we've ever had to face.' And Burden kept it to himself. We made the promise that he'd be the first told, when we finally got the guy. And he was very honourable about this. I think for a journalist that must have been a very difficult decision.

'De Vere Hotels had only just completed the purchase of the Grand,' says Bob Hamblyn, who, as a senior figure at construction firm Llewellyns, played a key role in the rebuilding of the hotel. He says that De Vere's had phoned the hotel's previous owner, to ask for advice, and were told to hire the architect Paul Treadgold.

Paul came to the site with his team, and started to look at what needed to be done, and what might have to be done. In the background were negotiations, which we were not part of, with the insurers. And, slowly, a plan started to form, and Longley's started to do the work. And they were about five or six weeks into the demolition and tidying up and trying to secure the site. And Paul Treadgold phoned me at the office.

Treadgold said something like: 'I'm not getting on with these Longley people at all. In fact I've fallen out with them in a very big way. Do you think that, if I managed to get Llewellyns involved in the project, would you run it? Could you say that you would run it?'

Hamblyn hadn't visited the scene at that point; he had no idea of the extent of the damage. 'We didn't know whether we were going to go and do two or three million pounds' worth of work, or what. We just didn't know. We had no idea. All we knew was that it was the highest profile construction project in the UK at the time. And we wanted a part of it.' So he said yes, without checking with any of his colleagues. But when they found out, they agreed he'd made the right decision. 'It was a no-brainer.'

Hamblyn says that Longley's and Llewellyns were invited to bid for the rebuilding contract, which would be done on a 'prime-cost fixed-fee' arrangement.

> [Because] you couldn't define the precise nature and extent of the works, you couldn't actually price it; you agreed to do the work, and they would pay you the cost of doing it, and a percentage on top. So what we had to do was bid for the percentage that we were doing.

Now, construction margins are very slim, and we thought that it was a big ask to actually overturn a contractor who was already there, and get ourselves on. So Llewellyns looked at it in a very holistic way, about, what are the advantages to the company, and the Llewellyn group as a whole for all the publicity we're going to get.

They would make some money by hiring their own machinery to the site, and a percentage profit on the quotes of subcontractors.

So there was a bit of a margin in there. So we talked about it, and we decided that we had to make quite a dramatic bid. And we bid minus half of one per cent as our margin. And they appointed us.

'My view was that the Grand Hotel had now become an icon to defiance of the IRA,' says Bob Hamblyn.

And I don't think it was ever, ever contemplated that it should be demolished. Actually, aside from the vertical section of the building, just inside the main entrance, and immediately to the right, the building was undamaged. So you had this core where a huge chimney stack was dislodged by the bomb. And it was several hundred tons of masonry, this chimney stack toppling, which thundered down between the walls and just snapped off the joists on the way.

But beyond that, the hotel was very much as it was. So the grand staircase was fine, the ballroom was fine, the kitchens were fine. All the rear bedrooms were fine. There was a big wing at the back, [which was] fine. I would say only 5 per cent of that building was seriously, seriously damaged, in the blast. But the damage was so significant, in terms of putting it out of use, that they would have been stupid not to have seized on the opportunity to rebuild the Grand, but rebuild it so that it looked the same on the outside, but was completely modernised on the inside. Which is what they did.

It was very quickly seen that the restoration of the inside and the restoration of the outside were completely different skills, and Paul Treadgold was going to be overwhelmed. So they wisely decided to appoint architects who would deal with the internal fabric of the building, leaving Paul to deal with the external, the historical side, of the project.

The hotel's owners appointed a third set of architects to

build a nightclub in the basement, Hamblyn recalls, and another team to build a multi-storey car park for the hotel.

The owners spent some time 'sorting out how they wanted to reconfigure the [interior],' Hamblyn suggests.

> But the beauty was that we could do things incrementally while they were still working out what they wanted to do to other parts of the hotel. So [there was] a very, very intense and complicated logistical planning regime. We had two full-time planners, planning engineers on site, and that's all they did all the time, was scheduling the work, how we overlapped this, what we did first, what we could do in parallel to keep the project moving.

Hamblyn describes it as 'a highly charged project', involving 'up to 500 operatives on site, at the peak', plenty of night shifts running, significant security precautions, and 'almost like a complete replica of our office' being established on site. 'We had a full-time site project manager, surveyors, secretaries, costing clerks. We put a whole panoply of staff over there to run this project. It was just huge.'

Waiting for Patrick Magee to resurface 'was awful', Detective Inspector John Byford says. 'He could have been anywhere in the world.'

'I think certainly there was an acceptance at senior officer level that there wasn't a lot more we could do, and that we had to let it take its course,' says DCI Graham Hill.

> All the intelligence was [saying] he wasn't over here, so in a sense we had to sit on our hands over this. And I think there is a level of frustration because, whether it was this inquiry or another inquiry, if you know who the person is and you're a bit hamstrung in doing what you'd normally do, like go out and find him.
>
> You can track people down, but you can't if it means crossing national boundaries, and particularly with some of the problems we would have faced had he been in southern Ireland, yeah. But, I wouldn't say... there was no anger or anything like that. I mean, frustration, yes, probably, because detectives are detectives, aren't they?
>
> You know what I mean, the psyche of a detective on a murder inquiry is, 'We've got to get this guy who did it.' And if it gets protracted and delayed, and obviously we're not aware of some of the measures, maybe, that are being taken to catch him. I mean I certainly wasn't, whether Jack Reece was, possibly he was. But, other than the fact that we

knew there was active work going on to try and
find him and to try and know what he was doing
or what he planned to do, we didn't know anything
really about what was going on across the water.
And I can understand why.

'We hadn't a clue where he was. No idea,' says Metropolitan Police surveillance officer Brian McDowell. 'Nobody
had any idea where he'd gone.'

After Patrick Magee had been identified as the key
suspect, he'd been found to be 'living openly' in Dublin,
according to a BBC documentary from 1986.[41] 'The police
took an enormous gamble. Fearing possible extradition
problems, they decided to wait and to watch,' in the hope
he'd come back to Britain. However, 'by June, the trail
was dead. The waiting game had failed.'

CHAPTER SIX

LET THE GUY RUN

In the early morning of Saturday 22 June 1985, a Metropolitan Police surveillance team were in Carlisle, waiting for IRA suspect Peter Sherry to come out of the hotel where he'd spent the night. When Sherry emerged, surveillance man Brian McDowell says, 'he went to a pub by himself, and he had a few drinks, and then he went back to the railway station. And that's where he met Magee.'

At the station, two members of the surveillance team were pretending to be a kissing couple.

> The easiest way to keep an eye on somebody if there's no cover is to have a kissing couple, or two

guys standing opposite each other, or two girls standing opposite each other, one looking at the subject and the other, as if they're having a conversation. That's when you've got no cover. The kissing couple was... what looks more natural? The thing is, you've always got to look as if you belong to where you are.

The previous night, McDowell and a colleague – who was one half of the kissing couple – had spent a long time looking at photographs of suspects together. She said, over their radio system, 'I think it's Magee.' They didn't know, at that point, what exactly Magee was suspected of.

'They said, "Right, Brian, off you go." Because I'm Northern Irish, you see. So they always sent me in. If there was anything to do with Irish, they sent me in. A) I can speak the language if I have to, and B) I understand them a lot better. And I'd been on the surveillance team quite a while. So they said: "Right, in you go, you confirm or not."'

The two suspects were in the station buffet. McDowell went in.

I saw him first, and then I started looking for the finger, because I knew he had part of his finger missing. [I] said yes, I'm 90 per cent certain – you never said 100 per cent – I said I'm 90 per cent certain it's Magee.

That information was fed back to Scotland Yard. The senior officer in charge, because it was a Saturday, wasn't as high-ranking as normal, because nothing ever happens at the weekend, as you know. He knew who this guy was and what he'd done, and how important he was, and he had to make a decision – do we arrest him at Carlisle, or do we let him run? And that was one of the bravest decisions a senior officer will ever make. He said, 'No, I have confidence in this team, I will let the guy run, and see where he leads us.'

Sherry and Magee got on a train towards Glasgow. Half the surveillance team got into cars and tried to get to Glasgow Station in time to take up their positions before the train arrived.

The weather that day was horrendous. It was one of the coldest Junes we'd ever had, and the people who drove there all deserved a George medal. Because it was lashing it down, and they were driving as fast as they could, because speed limits don't apply. They

drove as fast as they could to get to Glasgow, before
the train. Which was an HS125, so it's a fast train.
They got there, yes.

The surveillance team, still unaware that Magee was
wanted for the Brighton bombing, followed him and Sherry
out of the train station.

Basically they got on a bus and they were followed.
I'm not going to tell you about it, because I could
write a book on that bus journey, to be honest. But
factually, all you need to know is they got on a bus,
and they got off the bus, and were followed to that
tenement building where the flats were.

This was on Langside Road. The building contained seven
or eight apartments. 'We couldn't say which door, because
we didn't know,' McDowell says. 'If you follow people
into a block, it's very dangerous. So we followed him [to]
the block, and we kept observation on the block until the
local police arrived.'

Strathclyde officers waited 'all afternoon hoping they
would come out,' says Detective Chief Superintendent Ian
Robinson. 'You had to keep people on both sides, up and
down the street, you had to have at least two people there,

so that they could follow him. Probably more. And we managed to get into a house opposite, so we could look at the door.' People were seen coming in and out, but none of them were Magee or Sherry.

> It's getting into the afternoon. This is Saturday, in Glasgow, and to sustain this sort of operation over a long period, it's really very difficult. And I could see that we're going to have to do something.
>
> And the Met were getting a bit nervous about this, we're getting pressure – 'You'll have to go and do something about it, you'll have to get in there.' But I'd already reached that conclusion. So I got permission from one of the ACCs [Assistant Chief Constables] to issue firearms, because, this is an IRA lot, so obviously, the probability was that they would be armed. And, this was the dilemma. How do you go about this?
>
> There's two ways of doing it. The orthodox method is to get the SWAT team and go and root them out. But this is a [block] with eight [flats], so there's seven other flipping families in there. And, what's going to happen? So I decided that we would try and do it the quiet way, and, I put out a call. I didn't have enough firearms officers myself, because

you'd need one for each flat, I reckoned, that's eight up above. You probably need a couple on the street as well. So I'm looking for ten authorised firearms officers, on a Saturday evening in Glasgow. And plain clothes. So that's not easy.

So I put out a call, and the Serious Crime Squad responded. And I got my own officers, as many as I could. In addition to that, the main centre for terrorism suspects was the main central police office in Glasgow, Stewart Street, and this is on a Saturday night. It's one of the busiest police stations in the country.

And I had to arrange for, we were anticipating that we would have prisoners, so we would take over the whole police station, they had to transfer all the normal business to the northern police office. How in god's name the press never got hold of this I don't know. But anyway, they didn't.

And so I asked them to assemble, all these people I called out, at the southern police office, which wasn't that far from Langside Road. And I briefed them.

We put a man, one of the firearms officers, at each of the houses, and we arranged it [that] they would go in, and at a given signal they would rap every door, and they would say, 'It's a pizza delivery', or something like that, and, 'Oh, we've made a mistake'. So that's, in fact, what happened.

We didn't have pictures [of the suspects], and it wouldn't have been any use anyway, because it probably wasn't going to be Magee or Sherry who came to the door. We didn't know who was in the flat. So you just had to use, just had to suss it out. If there was any doubt, they were going to go in. I didn't have any warrants or anything, but if there was any doubt, they were going to go in, put it that way.

When all the doors were knocked, one was answered by Magee himself. 'He was seized by the arm, and thrown out of the house to other officers,' a 1986 BBC documentary noted. 'More policemen burst into the hallway. They had orders; everyone in the house had to be arrested.' Four other people were in the flat: Sherry, prison escapee Gerard McDonnel, and two women, Ella O'Dwyer and Martina Anderson.

'There was no resistance, they didn't try to shoot their way out, didn't make for the gun or anything like that,' Ian Robinson says. 'In the house, [officers] found £10,000. That was obviously what Sherry had brought across. And they took them into custody, took them to the central police office.'

There, Robinson made a point of going to see each of the five prisoners himself.

> I asked them if they had any complaints. None of
> them said anything. The only one who sort of smiled
> at me was McDonnel. They didn't say who they
> were, by the way, none of them said who they were.
> They refused to identify themselves at all. We knew
> who two of them were, and it was soon evident
> that McDonnel was an escapee, from prison. [We]
> had RUC officers across to try and identify them.
> They identified Anderson, I think, because she'd
> been arrested in Ireland for something else. But
> O'Dwyer hadn't been, and it was quite a difficult
> identification, on O'Dwyer. We didn't know who
> she was.

'There's always, on any major inquiry, a mix of euphoria and satisfaction, and "we did it!"' says DCI Graham Hill.

> [But,] of course, that's only the first stage of the
> process, because you've got to get through a close
> and very scrutinised trial. Although you're allowed,

I think, a degree of self-satisfaction, that very quickly
turns to, 'Right, now we've got the man, we've got
to prove [our case], and get a conviction in court.'

It might appear less exciting, but it has to be done.
You have to follow through all those other lines of
inquiry, to make sure you're not vulnerable when
you get to court. So yeah, it was very satisfying.
At some level, if you use the word euphoria, you'd
use the word euphoria. But very quickly you think,
'Right, this is only the first part done.'

And, actually, there was a more immediate problem. In
the flat in Langside Road, police found evidence of a plot
to plant sixteen bombs, in London and various seaside
resorts, during the summer. But, searching the flat, police
couldn't find the bombs. Where were they?

From a 'bomb calendar' found on one of the suspects,
police knew that one of the devices for the seaside terror
campaign had already been planted. The calendar said:
'First floor, 112, Front, Rubens Hotel, Buckingham Palace
Road'.

'The piece of paper they'd found had got other locations, just in terms of towns, with dates on, so it wasn't
clear whether the bombs in those places had been already
placed,' says Robin Butler, Thatcher's principal private

secretary. 'And whether we should give a warning, whether the warning might cause panic, and so on. It was a really difficult decision, about how we handled the question of a warning.'

'They called all the MPs [for those areas] in to New Scotland Yard and briefed [them],' Brian McDowell says. 'The MPs for the areas where there were bombs [planned]. So they did this nationwide search of all the hotels in all the resorts, all over the country. Because nobody knew.'

'From what we found in the flat, we were able to trace a guy in London. It turned out that he was a minor cog in the wheel,' Ian Robinson says.

This source, who hadn't been a particularly competent IRA member, and was later described as a 'reluctant recruit',[42] cooperated fully with Scottish Police. Robinson recalls: 'He told us that he had been to, or he knew of, a house where he'd seen them, and where he had knowledge that they had bombs.'

This house, actually a flat, was in James Grey Street, Glasgow. Officers visited it with a mechanical bomb sniffer. 'According to what I'm told, it went off the scale,' Robinson says.

> They thought that their machine they had was faulty,
> and there wasn't anything there at all. Well, they

searched the house, and in fact there wasn't anything there. But I wasn't happy with it at all, I thought, 'this information looks too good to be true'. I sent them out again, and two of the crime-squad fellows were searching a cellar. It wasn't locked, it was just a cellar, a coal cellar at the bottom of the close. And they found all these parcels.

They were wrapped in plastic, and completely wrapped with sticky tape. And, I think there was the correct number, [and] there was timers. And some of the timers were actually running. But there was no detonators, and we never found the detonators. They were obviously kept separately, for a good reason.

Officers took the bombs out of the cellar, and laid them out on the back garden. 'We got the bomb squad down, and I asked them, I said, later, "What would have happened if this lot had gone off?" And he said, "Well, you'd have had complete devastation for about 100 yards, collateral damage within 500, and minor damage within a thousand." It was an enormous amount of stuff.'

Though the 'bomb calendar' said which room the Rubens Hotel bomb had been planted in, 'they didn't find it the first time they went in,' surveillance man Brian McDowell says. 'They went in and said, "There isn't a bomb in this room." And we said, "There is a bomb in that room, go back and check it again."' It took them three hours to find it.[43]

'I think there were seventy or ninety wrappings of cling-film around the explosive,' says Alan Burt, who ran the Met Police's specialist search-dog team. 'The effort to stop it being discovered, by smell, from the dog, was tremendous, huge amount of work.' Eventually, when the bedside cabinet in the room was lifted, the bomb was found. The explosives officer said: 'Get out!' Burt recalls: 'Mostly impressed on my mind is my speed down Buckingham Palace Road.'

'Because he'd been arrested, we could then use his photograph,' detective Paul Gibbon says.

> We believed they'd been staying in a flat in Hackney somewhere. And so, we took the photographs round to estate agents, and an estate agent identified as having leased a flat to him in Hackney Road. So, we go raid this flat, and it was a top-floor flat – again, to my recollection – and underneath the floorboards, we found a gun, we found bomb-making equipment, in terms of a soldering iron, pliers, wires, various other stuff that you'd use for bomb making. We found a gun.

They also found a child's drinking flask. This was significant, Gibbon recalls, because it matched the lunchbox in which the Rubens Hotel bomb was found. 'And we also found a newspaper, with a crossword either finished or partially finished.'

When 'Roy Walsh' had given his nationality as English on his registration card, he'd written the capital 'E' with a distinctive diagonal line through it. Within the newspaper crossword that was found in the flat, there was an 'E' that had been written in the same way.

> So it was significant, finding the gear there, the gun, the bomb-making equipment, the flask as well, that was pretty eureka, but that didn't say that it was [Magee]. What did was finding that crossword puzzle. As a detective that's… You think, 'Yeah! I've scored the winning try at Twickenham.'

'I think there was a, always [has] been, as part of PIRA's tactics, implicit threat to companies who "cooperated with the crown", I think is the words that they would use,' says Paul Gibbon. 'The main airlines, the main airlines flying between Glasgow and London, did not want to carry [the IRA prisoners]. And the person tasked with finding a charter found it really, really difficult.' Once a charter company had been found, a group of officers went to Scotland to formally arrest them. Paul Gibbon was one of the two officers who arrested Magee. 'He said nothing. Looked at the wall,' the detective recalls.

Magee was taken to Paddington Green police station. There, Bernie Wells and Jack Reece could finally meet and interview the man they'd been after since January.

'Magee was wheeled in, brought in,' Wells recalls.

> Never opened his mouth. We asked all the pertinent questions. 'Have you ever been to Brighton? Do you know the Grand Hotel?' All the things you would ask, as a detective. He sat down, he looked at [the desk], and that's what he did the whole time. I bet you if, when he'd walked out, if you'd have asked him to describe us he wouldn't have been able to. He just sat there. Uncanny, almost. I was virtually 100 per cent he wouldn't talk. But I did expect that he might say, 'I'm not commenting.' Or, 'I've nothing to say.' He didn't say a dickie bird, from the minute they wheeled him in, sat him down, he never opened his mouth, at all. And as I say, he never looked at us.

Patrick Magee pleaded not guilty to five counts of murder, and not guilty to two other charges, connected to the Grand Hotel bombing. On 10 June 1986, he was convicted of all seven. For these, and for his role in the planned seaside-bombing campaign, he was given eight life sentences.

The police 'would never have a celebration before someone's been convicted and jailed,' *Argus* reporter Jon Buss says. 'They actually waited for him to be sentenced, and that was a couple of weeks after he'd been convicted. And then they had the celebration, which is the sort of celebration where some of the VIPs attend with their wives and everyone sips sherry, and then the VIPs and their wives go home, and all hell lets loose. It was one of those parties.'

'I met Margaret Thatcher, many years later,' says the detective Paul Gibbon. At a formal dinner, he told her about his role in the arrest of Magee. 'She put her hand on mine, she leaned forward and said, very, very quietly: "We got them in the end, didn't we, my dear."'

CHAPTER 9

PEOPLE DO THINGS DON'T THEY

CHAPTER SEVEN

PEOPLE DO RECOVER, DON'T THEY?

'I got myself out of hospital just before Christmas [1984],' says Norman Tebbit. 'I say I got myself out of hospital – I was pissed off with being in hospital.'

He decided to gate-crash a pre-Christmas party at the DTI building, which was being held to celebrate the success of the BT privatisation. 'It was my first occasion out of hospital, and it was quite painful actually in the car, to drive,' Tebbit says.

> I arrived there and went up in a lift, and as the lift stopped [and] the doors opened, it was clear that

there was a party going on, and a pretty good one.
So I stood at the door and shouted at the top of my
voice: 'So that's what you buggers get up to when
I'm not here, is it?' And I found it uncomfortable
to sit down and uncomfortable to stand up, so I got
my bum wedged on the edge of a desk, and said a
few words, and everybody seemed quite cheered by
it all, and it was, as I say, a very good party.

During Tebbit's time in hospital, his staff had been 'getting on with it. It was pretty impressive stuff, really,' says
junior minister Geoffrey Pattie. 'There wasn't any sort of
panic or "what on earth are we going to do?"'

Pattie doesn't recall any particularly strange atmosphere during Tebbit's absence, or a sense that people were
dwelling on it.

I don't quite know, if I had remembered it, how
would that manifest itself. If a chap suddenly broke
down at the end of a meeting and burst into tears,
or something, and I'd said, 'What's the matter with
you?' 'Well, I'm just so worried about the Secretary
of State.' I mean, nothing. People just went on doing
things. And I think really, the relief and the delight
when he came back at the BT [party] was as much

a sort of release of pent-up anxiety as anything else. But otherwise it wasn't manifest. I mean, I don't think you could have gone in off the street and thought, 'Golly, what's the matter with this place?'

On 10 January 1985, Norman Tebbit made his first post-bomb Cabinet appearance, and told journalists that he was looking forward to 'roughing up the Labour Party before too long'.[44]

Just before he returned to the despatch box, five days later, he felt:

that nervousness that perhaps a racing-car driver might have the first time he's on the starting line after having had a major accident. 'Am I quite as good as I was before I had this, these injuries?' I'd been out of the House of Commons for, what, three months. And there are not many records of people being out for three months and holding the same job and going right the way through, in that way. I don't know if there is or was a precedent for it.

'I was determined to demonstrate that I was the same old Tebbit, and certainly not looking for sympathy or a soft ride,' he notes in his autobiography. He says now that

'I don't think there was any element of [Labour] going easy on me, because I wasn't going easy on them. Normal service was resumed.'

As it was at the department, with what he calls 'our usual robust discussions'. His principal private secretary, Callum McCarthy, says that 'once Norman was back in the department, I can't remember it being in any way different'.

'It was just a steady [process] of getting back to work, and of learning to live with a certain degree of disability,' Norman Tebbit says.

> I was quite happy once I'd got back into the office, that I was coping OK with it. But of course, I had then no domestic life, obviously, apart from my visits out to Stoke Mandeville. And so I probably worked longer hours than I would normally have done.
>
> And most of the rest of the time I was in the House of Commons, because I didn't have anywhere else to go. I was living in a little flat over Admiralty House, which had a lovely view of the Parade Ground, and that was fine, but it was a bed-sitter, not a place where you particularly want to be. So I would either be at the department at work, or with my mates in the House of Commons, or I'd be out at Stoke visiting my wife.

I also, of course, had the additional company and support of my protection team. I'd had protection against the far left, on an on-and-off basis, when the boys thought it was necessary. But intelligence constantly showed that the IRA were of the view that they would profit greatly by finishing the job, and so my name was fairly high on the list of people who they wanted to murder. And I had a very good team. They were a right bunch of hoods [laughs]. And, of course, they went everywhere with me. If I went out for dinner, if I visited my family, whatever I did, I always had them with me. So that was an additional source of company. It was a curious life, until my wife came out of the hospital, which was quite some time.

'I think everyone was absolutely horrified by what had happened,' Callum McCarthy says. But the pursuit of business as usual 'wasn't a political statement, "we must show them that terrorism doesn't work", or anything. It was, "you have a job to do, get on and do it". If your printing press was blown up, you would be deeply irritated, but the reason why you would find another printing press is because it's your job to get newspapers printed.'

'Didn't give the IRA a thought, I'm afraid,' says his

colleague Brian Hayes. 'Apart from thinking what bastards they were.'

Ann Widdecombe, who had heard the explosion, says that:

> quite often in my mind, for about a year afterwards, I could hear the bomb. I'd hear it again, in very unexpected circumstances. I'd be vacuuming or something, and suddenly I'd hear the bomb. So I think it did have a pretty big impact, and other people have said similar things, who were close to it at the time.
>
> If I hadn't heard it, I don't think I would have been [affected]. But I heard it, and so, occasionally... I often used to think afterwards, that was the moment – I actually heard the moment that Jean Shattock died. Now, I know other people died, but she was the one who I happened to know. And that Margaret Tebbit was completely paralysed – I heard the moment it happened. I used to hear it again, as I say, in the most unexpected circumstances, when I wasn't even thinking about Brighton or the bomb or the Conservative Party, or anything else. That happened, I suppose, for about six months to a year.

'One of the police officers that was on the front door when the bomb went off, he retired on ill health, it was post-traumatic stress disorder, because of the bomb,' traffic officer Mike Rees recalls.

> I can remember seeing a photograph that he had of himself, he showed me once, where, although he was policeman shaped, he was dust coloured. He was just completely covered in dust by this bomb.
>
> About eight or nine years after the bombing, we were all sitting round having breakfast, before going to a fishing match, and the conversation got round to the Brighton bombing. And, after about thirty seconds of talking about it, and just in general terms, he got up from the table where we were all sitting and having breakfast. He got up, ran over into the corner and threw up. So even nine, ten years after the bombing, it had that much of an effect on him. That was the thing that not a lot of people recognise.

'The mind has a great capacity for shoving painful and unwelcome things out of the way,' Norman Tebbit says.

> It's a part of the defence mechanism. And I let that happen. So I was fortunate in that I'd got a

demanding job to do, and a lot of people helping me to get back to it. So there was plenty to fill my days, fill my mind, and I didn't get unduly introspective. And it was only quite a bit later, really when my wife came out of hospital, that I began to wonder whether it was fair on her for me to continue in a job that was so demanding, of time and concentration.

I think an awful lot of ministerial wives and husbands have found it quite difficult to cope with life because of the demands on their partners. And gradually I came to the conclusion that it wasn't fair on her, and made my decision that I wouldn't go on beyond '87, in the government. I couldn't stand down from the House of Commons in '87, because it would have been very untidy, to have been running the election campaign, for an election in which one was not a candidate. I didn't think that would look tidy, so I kept my thoughts to myself until after polling day.

'We all knew' that Tebbit could have been Prime Minister, his private secretary Andrew Lansley says.

[However,] the demands that ministerial office place on families and spouses are in their way greater than they are for the principal. And that is because, when you're the principal, the adrenalin pumps, you go off and you do things. When things are tough you kind of get stuck in and respond to it, and when the media have a go, you fight back. But the families just sit there and take it. And have to live with the consequences of it all. And Margaret Tebbit had to live with the consequences of it all. It's tough.

His life was absolutely kind of consumed by all of this, which is what tends to happen in politics. Norman and Margaret were married before he ever went into politics. She married an airline pilot. So that change makes a big difference. And then suddenly, with the injuries, he realised even more than anybody would ever normally do, what a price Margaret, his Margaret, was having to pay, for the fact of the life that he had chosen.

In that sense, the loss of his ambition was embittering, must have been. Clearly was. But the sense of responsibility he felt towards Margaret actually was the dominant emotion, because, from his physical point of view, he could have carried on in politics. I mean he did, in a way, carry on in politics, but he could have carried on in the frontline, and he didn't – he knew he couldn't.

'Yeah, he gave up everything, to look after Margaret, absolutely true,' says Fred Bishop, the fireman who led the Tebbits' rescue, and subsequently stayed in touch with them. 'He really stepped back to Margaret as his responsibility more than anything. But, yeah, "the Chingford Skinhead" – I can never imagine him like that now.'

'Well, people do recover, don't they?' Norman Tebbit says. 'After all, you think, between 1940 and 1945, the things that happened to people, they were not expected to go away and cry, they were expected to get back and get on with it. You know, just because you've lost your leg, it doesn't mean you can't fight, good God.'

Andrew Lansley says: 'I suppose Norman is very much of a generation that was used to the idea that they would generally focus on the practical rather than the emotional. And that would be him too. And remember, he was a pilot and he'd been … he'd crashed the Meteor [aeroplane].' This happened during his RAF service. Tebbit described it in his memoirs as 'a close brush with death'.

Lansley continues: 'He'd been through stuff before, and this was his attitude to this: he'd been through stuff before and he was going to get through this too. "Still playing with the casino's chips", as he would put it.'

'Well, it was not my first sight of the dreaded horseman,' Tebbit says.

And, I suppose even from childhood, being bombed, seeing the odd ceiling come down in the house and things like that, windows and doors blown in. You grew up during the war, being aware of the fragility of life, let's put it that way. And that was reinforced then by times in the air force, losing colleagues. I can remember being a pall bearer to two of my colleagues the same day – a double funeral. Which makes you aware of the fact that life is very tenuous.

I'd sum it all up, really, by saying that, having grown up through the Second World War, with the acceptance that being bombed is a routine matter – indeed, having spent the night in an air-raid shelter was not accepted as an excuse for not having done your homework. And then, through flying fighters, again, the same feeling, and particularly on an auxiliary squadron, where we were a band of brothers. We were chums, and we relied up on each other implicitly and absolutely, and we weren't expected to make fusses. And that, I think, was a good preparation for coming a bit unstuck in later life.

Journalists were trying to get Harvey Thomas 'all the time' to say that he was really traumatised by the two and a half hours he'd spent trapped underneath rubble in the Grand Hotel.

> And it was because they weren't interested in the facts. They were interested in making a story. And there's not a huge story in just being ordinary. I didn't get much shock and trauma. Because, well, one doesn't, does one? I mean, I've been blown up a few times. We had a bomb in Northern Ireland. And I was bounced out of my bed by another bomb in Northern Ireland, in the Europa Hotel. One gets on with it. I think it was important that I was not structurally injured. Cuts and bruises are fine, but I didn't actually break any bones.
>
> I went up one floor, through the roof, and down three floors. It was an extraordinary experience. Today they'd call it a traumatic experience, particularly since I'm a bit claustrophobic anyway. I like space, and to be totally confined and buried under ten tons of rubble is not pleasant. But I think the moment [the doctor] said to me, 'Oh, you have no bones broken,' I said – right, then, let's get on with it.

'Those huge stories have a natural cycle,' *Argus* reporter Jon Buss says.

It starts with the first two or three days, you're just writing about what happened, the shock of what happened. I remember walking past the Grand Hotel with my three very young children, about a week afterwards, and looking at the hotel, and I looked at it as a passer-by for the first time. And I was absolutely shocked at what I was seeing. The extent of the damage. It was open-mouth stuff. I was pointing it out to my little kids saying, 'Look, look at that!' And I'd been working on that story for a week. But I'd been in automatic mode. I'd just been finding out stuff, writing it up, printing it. Six editions a day, the paper. You would write something up, and it would be in the paper, on the streets, an hour and a half later. This wasn't like newspapers now. So it took a week for me to actually realise, personally, what had happened.

And when you're covering something like that, it always happens that you start the first few days reporting what happens. Then about day three, day four, the press turns on the police, and then they hunt like a pack. Everybody did it; it's all of a sudden somebody's fault. So fingers are pointed, and in this case it was towards Roger Birch, the chief constable, who didn't deserve it, but he was the victim of the finger pointing, nationally as well.

You work through that, and then other stories emerge, like the people recovering in hospital, and the investigation, all those bits and pieces. There's no decision taken to drop it. Journalists are very pernicious people; something better comes along, it kicks that story off the front page.

I think it was a couple of months later, there was a plane crash on the South Downs, near Eastbourne, and nine people died, in a small jet that was on a Beaujolais run. They were all Irish guys, they were Irish journalists, and that was a huge story. That kicked the bomb off the front page. But then that's the nature of journalism, isn't it? You keep bashing away at a story as long as the story's there, and then something comes along to boot it off the front page. And that's what happened.

'I hesitate to use the word fantastic to describe a tragedy where five people died and thirty-four were injured,' Jon Buss says. 'But we had the time of our lives. What a huge story.'

'It was an amazing story,' says *Argus* political reporter Adam Trimingham.

We had a discussion later as to whether it was the
biggest story that there'd ever been in Brighton,
and we decided it was. There'd been other things;
the town had been sacked by the French in 1514
and 1545, and there was the Second World War,
where 200 people, 200 civilians died. But that was
common to everyone in every town, really. This was
particularly a Brighton thing, and there'll never have
been anything bigger. The circulation that day was the
biggest that the paper ever had. It normally sold about
100,000 copies a day, but that day it sold 180,000.

In March, *The Argus*'s editor was named Journalist of the
Year at the British Press Awards. The judges said that the
paper's coverage of the bombing, and of the Ethiopian
famine, 'matched anything done by the national press'.[45]

Was it surprising, the extent to which things carried on
as normal after the bombing? 'Things always do,' Adam
Trimingham says. 'You always think, after a big story,
that never again things are going to be the same. But they
usually are.'

Sometime around early 1986, Bob Hamblyn recalls,
he and his team committed to a date by which the Grand
Hotel would be ready. The reopening ceremony was set
for 28 August 1986.

Because of the form of contract we were on, we were not hog bound by having to buy economically, or pay standard rates for labour. If we wanted people, if we wanted extra electricians or extra plasterers or whatever, and we couldn't get them, we'd just up the rate, we just paid the money and put the resource in. So it does show that it can work – that we committed to a date, and then as we worked through we could see that things were getting tight, we would throw money at it, basically, to get it done. Which is what we did.

We were on a four-line whip, really. Because we had to be finished. And towards the end of that project, Llewellyns had something like 500 operatives, workers, on site, overlapping with almost an equal number of hotel staff in training. So it was absolute bedlam through the final five or six weeks, with this overlap of construction crews and staff training.

We probably, towards the end, [had] a problem of exhaustion, of some of the site-management team, because the demands were really on them, they were working seven days a week. I know a number of staff cancelled holidays so they could get the project done. And Llewellyns, we paid for them to have a separate holiday, and some sort of compensation. Everybody wanted to make it happen. But there were a lot of very, very exhausted people at the end of it.

On the night before it opened, I didn't come home. I sat on a staircase, which was the last staircase which had to be carpeted, with a team of carpet layers, all night. They wanted to go home, and I said, 'When I go home, it'll show we've lost the will to finish this job. And I'm not going home. We've somehow got to get this done.'

And they worked all night, right into the following morning, and as Maggie Thatcher walked in, so the carpet layers were just coming out of the ladies' toilet, having laid the pink carpet.

At the reopening ceremony, Norman Tebbit joked to journalists about the time he spent buried in the rubble: 'Room service that night was slow. I had to wait three and a half hours before anybody came.'[46]

Mrs Thatcher's attendance that day 'was another nightmare for me,' Chief Constable Roger Birch says.

Because we'd still got IRA threats – no specific threats, but always the problem of [the] IRA. I'd been talking to the Home Office about this return.

[I] said it would be very helpful if it could be kept low key. So she had the band of Royal Marines, a flypast of Concorde, and god knows what. And I was there, of course, in uniform, and I had a mental note that if there was an IRA gunman somewhere I hope they shoot me and not her. The threat was… I was very glad when she got in her car and went away.

Despite the bomb and the brief slowdown it seems to have caused, Sir Robert Armstrong's talks with Dermot Nally were successful. Mrs Thatcher and her Irish counterpart Garrett Fitzgerald signed the Anglo-Irish Agreement on 15 November 1985. 'I think it's very natural, isn't it, that if you're engaged in a serious political process, you don't get blown off course by this kind of thing,' Armstrong says.

You have to pick yourself up and carry on. In that sense, I think she was quite right. If the Brighton bomb had been allowed to have a bigger effect on this process, the IRA would have won a point, which neither of us wanted them to win, neither the Irish nor we. And it was something you could do nothing about. You hoped that your security services would be sufficiently informed – as they were – to detect many of the outrages which were planned. You relied on them and carried on.

[Mrs Thatcher] made her speech the following afternoon as if nothing had happened. Or almost as if nothing had happened, because she referred to it. And just wrote it off as another IRA bombing attempt. There had been others, and there would no doubt be more.

'There were other planned attacks' on Mrs Thatcher by the IRA, Met Police surveillance man Brian McDowell says. 'I won't tell you what, but there was one very specific one. They checked a certain premises where she was definitely going to be, but their reconnaissance didn't go very well, so they probably aborted.'

Robin Butler, her principal private secretary from 1982 to 1985, is 'sure she was aware' of the general risk of another attack. But it was something that just went with the job. She left the security people to look after all that.

The time when it came up, as it were, most acutely, was the Dublin European Council in December, when the question was whether it was safe for Margaret Thatcher to go to Dublin. And it was decided that she should go, but that she wouldn't be able to move around in Dublin. So we helicoptered into Dublin Castle, where the European Council was taking place, and rather than go and stay at the ambassador's residence, which we'd normally have done, we stayed inside the Castle.

It was rather spooky being in Dublin Castle in the evening, because everybody had gone, and it was a great echoing empty place, when the other delegations weren't there. And I remember we had jokes about was it safe to turn on the television, or might it have been booby trapped, and was it safe to drink the bottle of whisky that had been put in the room. And in particular, Bernard Ingham and I were staying in a room which had a plaque on a wall about a man called Connolly, which said in this room he spent his last night on earth before being taken out and shot by the British. So, there was a certain amount of gallows humour about all that.

'No doubt we're all affected in ways that don't show particularly. But, if I describe my own reaction, I wasn't affected much by it,' says Robin Butler.

It was just one of the things that had happened. We were relieved and glad that we hadn't been among the injured. But apart from coping with the consequences of it in terms of how one looked after the injured – which obviously became quite a preoccupation over the next few days and weeks – we just got on with the job. I wouldn't even describe myself as shaken.

We were in a sense quite familiar with bombs. [At] that time, bombs were a pretty regular part of the situation. It was like any other bomb, in a sense, except that it had just been a bit closer.

Ann Widdecombe says:

You've got to put it in the context of the IRA atrocities as a whole. This was the biggest yet, but we were used to them. There were other atrocities, all the time. So, it wasn't just a one off, it was part of the IRA campaign.

You didn't have to be in government to be in danger from the IRA. And, we lived with it. If you were a Londoner you lived with IRA threats the whole time. Sometimes they were empty: buildings were evacuated, because there'd been a bomb warning but there was actually no bomb. Railway stations were a very favoured target for disruption.

Oh, there was a bomb at Waterloo, everyone has to be evacuated, the trains stop – oh, there's no bomb at Waterloo. We lived with it the whole time.

The risk of being bombed, Butler adds,

[was] one of these things you've got to accept as a fact of life. There's nothing much you can do about it. Take advice on reasonable security and all that, but having done that, you get on with it. And she did that. I don't think, either on her part or any of our parts, that this was a great sign of courage. You know, we just got on with it.

ACKNOWLEDGEMENTS

At an early stage of my work on this book, I had a dedication in mind. It was: 'For Alex Leith, who taught me to do journalism, and my parents, who played a more fundamental role.'

However, most of my gratitude has to be directed towards my interviewees. I possibly could have written a book without you, but it would have been very bad indeed. Thank you all.

Police officers

David Bard, Sir Roger Birch, Alan Burt, John Byford, Chris Cox, Frank Cox, Les Crabb, David Champion, Michael Colacicco, Brian Etheridge, Dave Gaylor, Andy Griffiths,

Paul Gibbon, Tony Gilks, Graham Hill, Les Jeavons, Richard Lovett, Albert Mariner, Brian McDowell, Roger Mead, Tim Mitchell, Allan Neil, Simon Parr, Paul Parton, Deacon Hilary Pownall, Mike Rees, Ian Robinson, Paul Solis, Mark Stanford, Mike Stone, David Tadd, Bob Thorn, Bob Trude, Paddy Tomkins, Bernie Wells, Bruce Wilson, and Andy Young.

Argus journalists

Jon Buss, Chris Oswick, Kate Parkin, Adam Trimingham, and Nick Turrell.

Fire service

Fred Bishop, Keith Ring, Paul Robb, Peter Rodgers, and Steve Tomlin.

Medical/hospital staff

David Bowden, Baroness Cumberlege, Pam Lelliott, Michael Forrer, Andrew Partington, Carlos Perez-Avila, David Skidmore, Simon Strachan, David Weir, and Chris Williams.

Politics/civil service

Lord Armstrong, Lord Butler, Sir Brian Hayes, Baron Lansley, Sir Callum McCarthy, Sir Geoffrey Pattie, John Powley, Lord Tebbit, Harvey Thomas, Dr Ruth Thompson, Sir Kenneth Warren, Ann Widdecombe, and Baron Wolfson.

Also

Prof. Ivor Gaber, Bob Hamblyn, John Henty, Charles Moore, and John Thompson, as well as others who provided information, or put me in touch with people: Graham Bartlett, Justin Bell, Bob Fenton, Peter James, Jan McCord, Phil Mills, Sir John Wells, staff at the Keep (particularly Christopher Whittick), and anyone else I haven't mentioned.

REFERENCES

1 Tebbit, Norman, *Upwardly Mobile* (London: Futura, 1989).

2 'To Kill the Cabinet', *The Argus*, p. 22. Available at The Keep, Falmer, BHBox 22/16.

3 This is Bishop's recollection of the conversation. A later report gives a more exact figure as to how many people were in the hotel when the bomb went off: 220 residents, thirty-two visitors, eleven staff, and ten police officers. See 'The Terrorist bomb attack on the Grand Hotel, Brighton – 12 October 1984', p. 24, which is part of Sussex Police Authority minutes, held at The Keep, Falmer (R/C 100/3).

4 Tebbit, Norman, (ibid).

5 Dale, Iain (ed.), *Memories of Maggie: A Portrait of Margaret Thatcher* (London: Politico's, 2000).

6 Millar, Ronald, *A View from the Wings* (London: Weidenfeld & Nicolson, 1993).

7   During his appearance on *Desert Island Discs* in 1992. Available at www.bbc.co.uk/programmes/p0093xdw

8   Moore, Charles, *Margaret Thatcher: The Authorized Biography* (London: Allen Lane, 2015).

9   See www.margaretthatcher.org/document/105577

10   Moore, Charles (ibid).

11   McAlpine, Alistair, *Once a Jolly Bagman* (London: Phoenix, 1998).

12   Aitken, Jonathan, *Margaret Thatcher: Power and Personality* (London: Bloomsbury, 2013).

13   See www.margaretthatcher.org/document/105574

14   On her *Desert Island Discs* appearance in 1996, available at www.bbc.co.uk/programmes/p0093nzl

15   Thatcher, Margaret, *The Downing Street Years* (London: Harper Press, 2011).

16   McAlpine, Alistair (ibid).

17   'I thought: Earthquake – but no, you don't have them in Brighton', *The Daily Telegraph*, 13 October 1984, p. 3.

18   Millar, Ronald, (ibid).

19   'Terrorists will not prevail, Prime Minister tells Tories', *The Times*, 13 October 1984, p. 4.

20   www.margaretthatcher.org/document/105763

21   www.margaretthatcher.org/document/105764

22   As she told a reporter from *Woman's Own*, a few days after the bombing (see www.margaretthatcher.org/document/105577).

23   'Tebbit tells of "feeling ragged"', *The Guardian*, 17 October 1984, p. 6.

24   Moore, Charles (ibid).

25 Silver, Roger (ed.), *Health Service Public Relations: A guide to good practice* (London: King Edward's Hospital Fund for London, 1985).

26 See, for example, 'Hairdryer triggers a bedroom alert', *The Argus*, 26 June 1985.

27 See Sussex Police Authority minutes from 5 October 1984, held at The Keep, Falmer (R/C 100/3).

28 See 'Extracts from the annual report 1984' in Sussex Police newspaper *Patrol*, available at The Keep, Falmer (BH701188.3).

29 'Inquiry on security blunder starts', *The Times*, 13 October 1984, p. 1.

30 See 'The Terrorist bomb attack on the Grand Hotel, Brighton – 12 October 1984', p. 24, which is part of Sussex Police Authority minutes, held at The Keep, Falmer (R/C 100/3).

31 'Timer clue to Brighton Bombing', *The Guardian*, 10 May 1986, p. 2.

32 See document SPA 10/63/2/3, held at The Keep, Falmer.

33 'Police take away 880 tons from bomb hotel', *The Times*, 31 October 1984.

34 Sussex Police Authority minutes, held at The Keep, Falmer (R/C 100/3).

35 This is all information from David Tadd, who gave a lengthy interview for this book, but preferred not to be tape recorded, and hence is not directly quoted.

36 'More jobs in service and leisure areas predicted', *The Times*, 5 November 1984, p. 2.

37 'The Brighton Bomb', *Patrol*, June 1986, p. 7.

38 This article is quoted in a document in the National Archives, reference Prem-19-1632.

39 'Police seeking second suspect for Brighton bombing', *The Times*, 18 April 1985, p. 3.

40 Burden, Peter, *How I Changed Fleet Street: Secrets from the Street of Adventure* (Leicester: Matador, 2011).

41 Accessed via www.youtube.com/watch?v=gmta9UIz5Dk

42 'Jail for bomb gang recruit', *The Argus*, 25 June 1986, p. 11.

43 'Thank God that IRA bombing plot was uncovered, jury told', *The Times*, 3 June 1986, p. 3.

44 'Tebbit back in Commons', *The Guardian*, 11 January 1985, p. 4.

45 'Bomb coverage wins editor top award', *The Guardian*, 29 March 1985, p. 2.

46 'Thatcher returns for a Grand reopening', *The Guardian*, 29 August 1986, p. 2.